ADVANCED PRAISE FOR *COMMON SENSE HAPPINESS*

"Wow, what a wonderful book! At first glance *Common Sense Happiness* appears to be a simple book filled with no-nonsense reminders of how to create your own happiness. The power of the book, though, is in the delivery. Loree has such a compelling, conversational way to help you to see the truths you have known all along, but may have forgotten or talked yourself out of doing."

As you read the book, you will feel like you have a powerful life coach sitting right next to you, ready to meet you where you are and committed to supporting you into YOUR own personal definition of happiness. Loree could be described as an 'in-your-face-hold-nothing-back' kind of coach. The same can be said of her book; when Loree invites you to "Stop whining, bitching and suffering' she means it. Don't open the cover of the book unless you are ready to step up to a new level of self-discovery and self-commitment."

~KC Miller, Founder/Director, Southwest Institute of Healing Arts

"Loree has created an easy, charming, direct approach to loving your life and creating happiness, no matter who you are or where you are in your life. Loree took 5 simple principles one by one and then introduced new thoughts to drive them home in an honest, colorful, fun and exciting read. No matter where you are in your life, you will find many nuggets and jewels to ponder and chew on in Loree's *Common Sense Happiness* book.

As I was reading, I kept thinking of all the clients and students who can benefit from Loree's book. You will too!"

~Richard Seaman, Master Life Coach, teacher, speaker, and Founder of Seattle Life Coach Training, and author of the books *It's All in the Sharing* and *Spiritual Reliability*

"After reading *Common Sense Happiness* and Loree's 5 Life A-Mazing Principles, I felt like I had been snatched in the collar by life. The KISS factor slowed me to a pace to ponder, go within, and truly visit my deepest wishes.

Loree, you are right on with 'life is both too long and too short to be anything less than what you want it to be.' Thank you for assisting me in peeling another layer off and seeing myself with new eyes."

~Yvonne "Jett" McFadden, ABR SFR eCertified Realtor

"Common Sense Happiness is a great read. It is inspirational and motivational as well as filled with simple solutions, which will make you feel good about yourself and your life. Everyone should read this book and create a more positive outlook!

"As the leader of a women's fundraising group, I found *Common Sense Happiness* enlightening, useful, and very uplifting. It gives the reader a simple path to follow that helps one make positive decisions. This book will delight you while leading you to very productive solutions for whatever problems confront you. Loree Bischoff will help the reader define and conquer any problem that comes along.

"Loree has the natural ability to make things so simple and clear. *Common Sense Happiness* helped me see that the answers and understanding I sought were always right there in front of me. It's like she already knew my life and could see the whole picture."

COMMON SENSE
HAPPINESS

5 PRINCIPLES FOR PEOPLE WHO WANT TO STOP WHINING, BITCHING AND SUFFERING

LOREE BISCHOFF

Love Your Life

Love Your Life

Love Your Life Publishing
7127 Mexico Road Suite 121
St. Peters, MO 63346
www.loveyourlifepublishing.com

ISBN: 978-1-934509-42-5
Library of Congress Control Number: 2011938739
Printed in the United States of America
First Printing 2011

Cover and internal design: www.Cyanotype.ca
Editing by Gwen Hoffnagle
Author Photos by Kathy Singer

why you want this
BOOK

Life is both too long and too short to be anything less than what you want it to be. If you have a long life in store for yourself, why on earth would you settle for unhappiness year after year after year? Why would you accept being sad and crabby for seventy-seven years (the average lifespan for Americans)? On the other hand, if a brief experience on this planet is what's in store, well, I wouldn't want to squander any precious time being a grumpy martyr.

Either way you look at it, there's just no good reason to spend a whole lot of time being miserable, unfulfilled, mad, or less than happy.

Still not sure if you qualify for a disposition overhaul? If you answer yes to any – even just one – of the questions below, it may be time to pause and figure some things out.

- Are you unhappy even when you're having fun?
- Are other people the reason you're crabby and unhappy?
- Do you think you're not educated enough or rich enough to have a happier life?
- Do you always feel like a supporting cast member in someone else's life?
- Do you have a negative belief about yourself that was established by someone you used to think was (or still think is) smarter than you?
- Are you just wanting something – anything – to change?

This book will help you do just that.

DISCLAIMER: Once absorbed, this book may cause expanded thinking, personal growth, direction, feelings of being in control, happiness, transformation, an uncontrollable urge to have an amazing life, and an unquenchable desire to evolve to something greater. You may also experience moments of unusual clarity and a newfound sense of well-being. Should these symptoms persist, all I can say is – GOOD.

CAUTION: Enlightenment can be highly addictive and is often contagious. Once exposed, it is almost impossible to get rid of, and more often than not the craving for more grows stronger over time. A certain percentage of people seem to be mysteriously immune, some people are mildly affected, and many report that positive, life-altering activity occurs.

DEDICATION

I would like to dedicate this book to YOU!

If you are preparing to turn this page and see what comes next, then I was right in dedicating this book to you. It has landed in your lap for a reason, at just the right time.

Is there ever not a right time to grow, to consider a new possibility, or to get a little happier? Let's see how it sounds if you answer yes:

Yes, it's not the right time for me to grow.
Yes, it's not a good time for me to consider a new possibility.
Yes, this is totally a bad time for me to try to get a little happier.

Wow – I'd kick my own ass if I heard myself seriously thinking these thoughts. Yet often many of us have those very thoughts, cleverly disguised as outdated beliefs, closed-mindedness, and the curious conviction that once we've made our bed we absolutely must lie in it! That just doesn't make any sense to me at all!

So, I humbly dedicate this book to you, and it's my sincerest desire that by reading it with an open mind and an attitude of willingness, you will learn that you can actually be happier.

"When one door of happiness closes, another opens; but often we look so long at the closed door that we do not see the one which has been opened for us."

❋ HELEN KELLER ❋

table of
CONTENTS

FOREWORD
by terry 'hulk hogan' bollea

You Don't Have to Go Through Any More Hard Times
to Be Happy

The interesting thing about Loree Bischoff is that she has so much brilliance packed inside her. I've known Loree as a friend and colleague for a long time and had no idea that she was such a gifted writer and artist. *Common Sense Happiness* is not only a great read, it is full of deep wisdom and spicy meatball sauce that makes you sit up and realize this book will change you. Life and joy live on every page of this book.

You may be surprised to hear someone in my line of work talking about living a life of peace, love, and joy. Listen, all the fame and money in the world can't buy you happiness.

Over the past five years, I've been on a quest. I've studied religion, spirituality, science, and psychology in an effort to understand my life and make it better. I wish I'd read *Common Sense Happiness* first. This book puts together the most important truths people need to know to be truly happy. When you read it, you'll be able to make sense of what you already know, stop the old patterns of thinking and behavior that keep you stuck in misery, and change your life completely.

You don't have to go through any more hard times in your life. You have suffered enough. We all have.

Let me cut to the chase. It's time to stop depending on the future for your salvation or dwelling in the past with your sob story. Knock that off. Use the information in this book to get yourself firmly into NOW, this present moment. Follow the steps that Loree presents so clearly in this awesome book and wake up to the fact that you can be happy, peaceful, and abundant.

Read this awesome book. Follow the five simple principles and apply them to your life. No matter who you are or what challenges you face, this book will help you move past negativity and move into the beautiful life you deserve.

The choice for happiness is yours…"Whatcha gonna do?"

Terry 'Hulk Hogan' Bollea
Clearwater Beach, FL
August, 2011

INTRODUCTION

This book is meant for those who may be new to the idea that we ourselves have control over our state of happiness. For you who have yet to put your toe in these waters and see how it feels, I invite you to come on in – the water's fine!

None of the concepts in this book are new. They have been spoken of and written about for thousands of years by countless others who were and are far wiser than I. This is just my way of delivering some of these age-old concepts in what I hope are a few simple, easy-to-understand principles that can help you start creating a happier life. I must warn you, though, I don't like to sugar-coat things. To be perfectly honest, my delivery, I'm told, is "lovingly blunt." That's the way I coach and that's what my clients expect from me. Just thought I should give you a heads-up.

Got a toe in? Okay, let me introduce myself. My name is Loree Bischoff. I am a life coach. As a life coach, my mission and my passion is to help you accomplish and experience *your* mission and passion. What I've found is that most people's mission boils down to one thing: being happy. And there are infinite ways in which people try to accomplish that, mostly by trying to add or eliminate something or someone to or from their life. That's one approach. I have another in mind, though, that I call the Life A-Mazing Principles.

Is your life amazing or just a frustrating maze? Do you keep repeating the same behavior and patterns and then wonder why nothing ever changes for you or why you feel unhappy or unfulfilled? Wish you had a little more control over your life?

Would you go to a buffet and deliberately put food on your plate that you know you don't like or are allergic to? Would you frequently let another person choose your food, regardless of your preferences, and pile it on your plate? Would you go back for seconds, thirds, and fourths of such foods? Now let's take it one step further. Would you then get angry at and blame the cook for placing those choices in front of you? Probably not. You would likely choose foods you like and stop eating foods you don't like or have an adverse reaction to. You certainly wouldn't hold the cook accountable for the choices you made. So why should the choices you make in other areas of your life be any different? Who are you holding accountable for the way you experience your life?

The Life A-Mazing Principles are about the realization that we have choices – every second of every waking moment. I like to look at life as a giant maze. But here's the big aha: We have to accept or at least be willing to consider that we create the maze as we go. We weave our way through our lives taking rights and lefts, moving forward and sometimes (seemingly) backward, and going over, under, around, and through people, places, and experiences. What an adventure! Each of us has a life maze and, like snowflakes, no two are exactly alike, even though they intersect, become entwined, and influence and affect each other.

I feel that we can all make choices that help make our lives amazing in our own unique way. That's why I was inspired to write this book. I love the maze of my life and it is my sincerest desire to help you love yours, too. My life maze has been created by many of the same ups and downs, good times, tough lessons, joys, and sorrows as other people's mazes. Many of the things my clients have experienced or are struggling with, I've experienced, too. I was one of two children, with a lower-middle-class upbringing. My parents divorced when I was a teenager, I dropped out of high school when I was a senior, and I watched my father survive a risky surgery to remove a tumor the size of a lemon from his brain and then proceed to drink himself to an early grave. Those same life experiences have a very detrimental effect on some people – often long term. Me? Somehow I just skipped right on through. Even through stressful and sad times, I managed to remain a happy person.

The difference is in how we view those things, how we let them affect us, and what we decide to do with them from here on out. I've learned to wake up and appreciate the opportunity that each day brings to choose how I want to be and how I want to create my maze as I journey through my life. I've come to understand that it's my life, my maze. I own it. I get to decide if I want to go left, right, over, under, plant a flower, plant a flag, build a retainer wall, tear one down, invite someone in, or just sit still for a while.

The maze of your life has been and will continue to be created, even if you aren't aware of it. It's happening anyway, so you might as well decide whether to actively participate or simply let it happen by default. You could just ride it out, letting other people and circumstances dictate your path. I personally don't enjoy being a passenger in my own car. I'd much rather be the driver, deciding where I want to go and what route to take to get there.

Not feeling that your life is amazing just seems like such a wasted opportunity. I mean, isn't that the point of being here – to create something that makes you happy, something that is your own special brand of amazing?

But just what *is* an amazing life, anyway? Let's start with what it is not. It is not based on fame, fortune, or a fancy title. Honestly, you can't qualify it in specific terms because it's subjective. Like they say, one person's trash is another person's treasure, or in this case, one person's "amazing" is another person's "huh?"

I remember living in a tiny studio apartment in downtown Chicago (pre-children) and trying to hold my breath every time I got on the less-than-pleasant-smelling elevator. Thank God I never got stuck in there with whomever was contributing to that scent. Talk about living in the moment – we barely had two nickels to rub together and our biggest concern was what bar had the best happy hour food. But hey, it was Chicago in the early '80s, and my husband (then boyfriend) and I were having a ball – stinky elevator and all! We went from there to living in two different houses, in ongoing battles to maintain ownership, as the mice were trying to declare eminent domain. I gave them a good run for their money, but they ultimately kicked my ass. We moved. I remember later on struggling to make the $350 per month rent payment, eating a lot of noodles, bouncing checks to buy diapers, and stressing over money much of the time. But I was with the love of my life, we had two beautiful babies, and in spite of navigating our way through starting a family and trying (not very expertly) to pay the bills, we were still happy! We were having a blast, completely unaware of the combined life maze we were creating.

Then my mom put a book in my hands that really lit me up (thanks, Mom) and put me on a path that would change my life. (It was by Catherine Ponder, and all of her books are fantastic.) Not in a big, dramatic, obvious way, but it provided a critical shift in thinking that at once gave me the best feeling I think a person can have: FREEDOM. Yep – that's it – the great life-changer for me was learning that my personal environment – my life maze – and my state of happiness were a product of my thinking and the actions and attitudes that stemmed from it. To me that spells

F-R-E-E-D-O-M. You see, I learned that how happy I was going to be, in any circumstance, shouldn't be contingent upon anyone else – only me.

Once I realized that if I wanted something more or different I had the freedom and therefore the power to try to create it, I had connected the dots. I had been doing that unwittingly every now and then, but now I was doing it ON PURPOSE. I started to learn how to control my thoughts, and therefore my emotions, so that I could consistently be happy under even stressful and trying circumstances.

The freedom to choose how we feel about any given situation is a freedom we all have. When someone says, "I can't help the way I feel," or "I can't change the way I feel," I wonder, "Really? You really can't? Are you absolutely, positively sure about that?" It's all good if the result is that you feel good, but if your thoughts and focus are making you feel bad, then wouldn't you want to get good at changing them to ones that help you feel better and more in control of your happiness?

How you choose to think and feel about things determines how happy or miserable you are. Even when my husband and I were flat-ass broke and in the fast lane to bankruptcy, I never felt poor, that it was someone else's fault, or that it was something I couldn't change. I just figured, "Well, I'm going to get up every day anyway and help figure out how to get to the next best place regardless of whether I'm happy or miserable, so I might as well be happy while I'm doing it."

All of the periods of my life have been amazing – each in their own, unique way, although I didn't always realize it at the time. As I look back, though, I can see how the choices I made – good and bad – were each another brick in the foundation and design of my life's maze. They made me who I am *now* and helped determine what I have chosen to BE in this life. Just as important, my choices have made me who and what I am *not*.

That life is amazing is demonstrated by the simple fact that you get to be here and you get to play it. If you don't like the maze you've created, or even if you don't agree that you've created your life maze up to this point, you can still change your view and redesign your maze if you really want to.

Having an amazing life is in large part recognizing that we wake up each day and choose how we feel about what we have already created and what we have experienced. We choose what we continue to create. We choose how we will feel about it at every moment and can make changes at every moment. Again – FREEDOM.

You can start to have an amazing life by acknowledging that you are here for a purpose and maybe that that purpose is to simply create a life that makes you happy. Period. There's no need to get caught up in how significant you think your life is or how it appears to others. Your purpose belongs only to you.

What trips your trigger and gets you excited about waking up each day is unique to you. It could be that building model airplanes or skyscrapers gives you the greatest sense of joy; it could be growing a garden or a family; or maybe it's volunteering to cook for the needy or being a professional chef. Maybe you're a goal-oriented person or maybe you just take life as it comes. If you're like most of us, the things that fulfill you change as you change and your experiences broaden. However you decide to realize your purpose – whatever you find fulfilling – that's what will make your life amazing to you. The beauty of this is that there is no one definition or idea of what an amazing life is. You get to construct your own maze, tailored just for your life and the way you want to journey through it.

✿   ✿   ✿

This book is about five simple, common sense principles that have been instrumental in helping me create a very fulfilling life that never ceases to amaze me. They've shown me that everything that has occurred has contributed to my growth, that the Universe/life/God has placed certain things in my path to *cause* me to grow, to become wiser, and to strengthen my constitution. As I look back at my journey through life to this point, I can see how I've shed and outgrown immature ways of thinking and behaving. I can also see how my weakest links have become stronger, and I know that because of the strength of my constitution I can embrace any situation that may arise, knowing it will contribute in some positive way to my life maze. That is the premise from which I coach my clients and that is what I hope will serve you well, too.

By being open-minded and giving the five Life A-Mazing Principles your consideration and sincere intention, you, too, can seize your own life maze and create a happier and more fulfilling life — one that just might amaze you.

a very brief snapshot of my
LIFE MAZE

1961: July 4th – I was born! So fitting to be born on Independence Day, as I cherish the belief that every soul should have the freedom to fly as it suits them.

1966: At the age of five, Mom signed me with an agency and I began modeling.

1966-1979: School years. I never liked a single day. Not even one. It became glaringly apparent during these years just how much I strongly disliked having someone else schedule my day – especially when I thought they were filling it with so much irrelevant and unproductive material.

My most memorable school days:

❋ My 9th grade teacher gave a homework assignment to write down what we wanted to be when we grew up. I was about fifteen and had absolutely no clue, and even if I had, I saw no reason to share this with a class of my teeming-with-bad-judgment adolescent peers. I refused to participate. My teacher asked me if I thought I was too special to do the assignment. No good answer – yes I'm too special or no I'm not special? I called in the big guns: Mom! Mom rocks. She saw my point and had a chat with the teacher. I love you for that, Mom. It would be about twenty-five more years before I figured out what I wanted to be.

❊ My 11th grade gym teacher caught me coming in late to school – again. I had no first period class, so really, where was the logic? She told me I would never be able to keep a job. I didn't have the heart to tell her that I'd been working since I was five, currently had two jobs, not only had I never missed a day but was chronically early, and I made more money at one of those jobs in an hour than she did in half her work week. That would have been mean. She just didn't understand me and that's okay – I didn't need her to.

1979: Senior year, and I decided it was time to stop wasting my time, so I dropped out at the end of the first quarter and got my GED. I just wanted to work more and get on with the adventure of life!

1984: I got married to the man of my dreams. I read a great romance novel when I was in my teens and fell in love with the hero. I decided I would marry a man like that character some day. And I did. Although he's a Gemini, so it's like being married to two men. But not to worry – I got this.

1984 & 1985: Oh – babies! Okay, let's do that now!

1984-2003: The years of parenting and creating our family life – an amazing, fulfilling journey filled with all the usual aspects, changes, and challenges that are life: growing, moving, adjusting, raising little people, family medical scares, losing parents, job changes, etc. But the constant was always lives filled with love and maintaining focus on the target.

2006:   By now my passion had revealed itself. All I could think about was how to help others create more fulfilling lives, so my sister and I began creating a motivational event for mothers which took place in 2007. This was the launch-point of my career as a life coach. My passion to help moms grew to include coaching those seeking to evolve and enhance their lives.

2011:   Completed and published my first book: *Common Sense Happiness*!

PRINCIPLE 1

HAPPY:
to be or not to be?

"When I do good, I feel good. When I do bad, I feel bad. That's my religion."
ABRAHAM LINCOLN

THOUGHT 1:
LET'S CUT TO THE CHASE – I JUST WANNA BE HAPPY

Okay, I confess; coaching and writing this book really is a completely selfish endeavor. The reason I became a life coach is that I love to learn what makes people tick and why they do the crazy, wonderful, illogical, bizarre, hurtful, and loving things they do. Then I love to try to help them enhance their lives. For me there's no better feeling than the one you get when you help someone come to a realization, discover what they're capable of, uncover new options, feel good about their life, and feel the joy of discovering new ways to make it even better. It's what makes ME tick. The good news is that by being selfish and indulging in what makes me happy, I get to be of service to others, so it's a win-win situation.

It can be tricky figuring out the difference between enjoying something or someone and expecting to be constantly provided with happiness and fulfillment from something or someone. I can happily enjoy a bowl of ice cream, but I don't expect it to fill a void in my life or provide me with lasting happiness. Yet that is exactly what we so often do: try to find happiness, peace, fulfillment, relief, ease, or freedom from suffering in a source outside ourselves. But you can't heal an internal condition or conflict or fill a void with an external band-aid.

As a life coach I see people struggling with this all the time. They're unhappy with their health, weight, or relationships; they want their partner to change or they want to be free of their partner; they're unhappy with the business they're in or because they're not in the business they want to be in; they're carrying around lots and lots of baggage; or they live in fear of losing something or someone or of being judged. So they use band-aids. Band-aids come in many forms: food, alcohol, drugs, constant compromise, procrastination, distractions, buying stuff, giving up too easily – things that cover up what's causing unhappiness and offer temporary relief, but don't actually fix anything or address the core reasons for the unhappiness.

If we constantly expect a happy life to come to us from something or someone "out there," we will never be able to achieve true, lasting happiness. At the heart of the matter, isn't that what we all want and crave? We just want to be happy, damn it! We all just want happiness, but we keep going the long way around to find it.

Learning how to be happy, regardless of the "somethings" or "someones" in our lives, is what we want to strive for.

THOUGHT 2: EXTERNAL FIX FOR AN INTERNAL JOB?

All we need is a little more money, our fifteen minutes of fame, and a few more possessions to be in Happyland, right? Not necessarily! Money, fame, and material things alone are not insurance policies for lasting happiness. They are external things to be used, experienced, and enjoyed. The media reveals to us on a daily basis people of fame and wealth who appear to have it all, yet their lives are a massive mess, often tragically so.

We are conditioned to believe that material things and people will make us happy. We are inundated our whole lives by sources all around us saying, "If you buy this car, if you own this house, if you vacation at this resort, if you look like this, have a partner like that… YOU WILL BE HAPPY!" But true happiness and fulfillment is an INTERNAL job, not an external one. Cultivating happiness from within will set you free. It's actually a shortcut. Why spend decades of time and tons of miles riding emotional roller coasters trying to get from outside sources what is already within you? And there's a bonus: You don't have to give up control of your state of bliss to find it. You remain the puppet master of your own, fine self. No one else can pull your strings and yank your chains!

THOUGHT 3: FILLING THE VOID WITH STUFF DOESN'T WORK

Can you find as much joy in sitting around drinking coffee with a friend, being by yourself with nothing to do, or washing your car as you can jetting to the luxury vacation of your dreams? Your initial response may be that the luxury vacation would be more joyful and therefore make you the most happy. It's sure to bring you relaxation, fun, adventure, and new experiences. All these things should make you feel… what? A sense of satisfaction? Feeling good and satisfied makes us… happy.

But if you are not happy before you go on your luxury vacation, all the joy and happiness you derive from that experience will only be temporary. If you are trying to fill a void with it, the results won't last and the void will return, demanding to be filled with something else, something more. Feeling like there is a void in your life and trying to fill it with things, food, drama, or a multitude of other choices that distract you from what the real source of your feelings is will never bring you lasting happiness. Eventually those things will cease to fulfill you and you will look for more things and then there's that cycle again. It isn't likely that you will feel happy and satisfied for long by trying to fill yourself up with material or superficial things. It will never be enough.

There's no denying that a luxury vacation is a delightful experience, but it's temporary, so it's not the answer to feeling fulfilled and finding lasting happiness. Enjoy it, appreciate it, and have a wonderful time. Soak it all up. But learning how to enjoy your life under *any* circumstances, whether vacationing, washing your car, or just sitting alone watching the rain, is how you win inner, lasting happiness. If someone is miserably unhappy before they go to Disneyland – The Happiest Place on Earth – Mickey Mouse, maid service, and all the caviar and champagne they can consume won't change that for long.

THOUGHT 4: YOU COMPLETE ME – ALMOST SOMETIMES

Most of us have at some point in our lives expected other people to provide us with happiness. Where relationships are concerned, we have this idea that we can become happy, whole, or complete only with another person by our side.

The notion that another person can or should be the only source of your happiness is a false notion. Do we deserve to be showered with efforts by our significant other to fulfill our needs? Yes, we do. Should we want to provide happiness and fulfillment to our loved one and strive to fulfill their needs? Absolutely. But there's a difference between graciously receiving and relishing in these gifts and expecting them to be our one and only resource for making us feel whole and complete.

Each of us has to figure out what our individual needs are and what really makes us happy. It requires some self-examination to learn what motivates you to think and behave the way you do. What exactly are you trying to accomplish? Are the methods you're using working for you? If *you* don't know, how on earth is someone else supposed to figure it out? They would likely never get it right! It may seem like they are fulfilling you for a while, but there will come a time when they disappoint you. Then what? The person you once considered to be the source of your joy has now become, at the very least, a disappointment, and worse, a source of misery.

Seriously, think about this! Are you stuck thinking that the only way to be happy and fulfilled is to have it provided for you by another? "If only I could just find my soul-mate, he would make me happy." "If only she could make more money, I would be happy." "If only he appreciated me more, treated me better, changed…, then I would be happy." "If I could just have a bigger house, a better job…" Any of that sound familiar? If you are in the habit of constantly handing over the care and nourishment of your emotional well-being to others, your happy meter will remain at the mercy and whim of the rest of the world. You're also delaying your happiness until some time in your future; you hope the current love of your life will eventually understand you, change to become the person you imagine they could or should be, or some other circumstances will change, and then you will be able to be happy! When we do this we discard

28

the chance to be happy right now. And now is the time that really matters. It's the only time that actually exists.

When we attach ourselves to the idea that happiness and fulfillment only comes to us through outside sources, we give up control of our own joystick. Don't misunderstand what I'm trying to say here. Having someone you love by your side is more than wonderful – it can be absolutely blissful – as long as it's not because you feel you are incomplete without that person or that you are incapable of providing yourself with what you really need to be happy. Not to mention that it's a lot of pressure for the other person.

In a nutshell it all boils down to this: it's all about the giving, not the getting. When your focus stays on the giving, everyone wins. The more we give to ourselves in the form of love, understanding, opportunity for growth, and the responsibility of holding ourselves accountable for our choices, the more of a complete and balanced person we are capable of being in a relationship. And the more we give to that special someone, the more fulfilled they become. We all know how great it feels to give a gift to someone. The gift of contribution (without strings), in just about any form, is one of the most fulfilling actions we can take. When we give without conditions, we also give to ourselves, so we automatically get.

What do we get? We get the privilege of helping to fulfill our significant other. We get to feel our heart swell – the physical sensation of love in motion – because we know in some way we've contributed beyond ourselves. That's a very complete and fulfilling state to be in.

THOUGHT 5: LEARN AND PRACTICE

So how do we get good at making ourselves happy? The same way we get good at anything – we LEARN AND PRACTICE, LEARN AND PRACTICE, and then we LEARN AND PRACTICE some more. Just like doctors practice medicine, lawyers practice law, singers practice singing, skiers practice skiing, etc. The best are good at being the best because they focus on and practice being and doing their best.

You've been practicing, too. You've been practicing to be the way you are now your entire life. So by now you are really good at it. Your processes and procedures are deeply engrained habits and patterns. If you think you can change how you think, act, and respond over a weekend, you will likely be disappointed. You can, however, get a hell of a good start in a weekend if you want to badly enough! Just remember, it's a process. As you pick up new ways of thinking and behaving, you must continue to consistently practice incorporating them into your life. Don't get mad at yourself and give up if you occasionally fall back into old patterns, thinking you'll never be able to change. You'll develop the awareness to recognize what you did and then you'll have a choice: keep practicing, or give up, stop growing, and stagnate.

THOUGHT 6: STOP

Sometimes I have my clients start by practicing how to STOP.

1. Stop resisting things (and people) we can't change.

2. Stop pursuing things (and people) that are not in our best interest.

3. Stop wasting good energy by thinking painful and frustrating thoughts about all of it.

It's amazing how much grief we cause ourselves by agonizing over the state of other people's lives and things we cannot change. Just let go of those things, give yourself some relief, and leave the stuff that's out of your jurisdiction or control alone, already!

It's easy to fool ourselves into thinking that other people's lives and affairs are our business (especially with family and close friends). They're not. Not any more than our business is theirs. That's just another way to distract ourselves from dealing with our own stuff, or to fill our need to feel connected or important. That's not to say we shouldn't care about those people and be concerned about their well-being; of course we should support them, love them, try to understand them, and help them if we can, as long as we can do it without judgment or strings attached. But other than that, we should tend to our own business and let others tend to theirs. We should STOP judging, STOP criticizing, and STOP thinking we know what everyone else should be doing with their lives – that's just arrogant. We don't know squat about another's path. What seems to us like an awful situation may be exactly what that person is supposed to be going through for their own soul's evolution. Practice stopping the pattern of judging things good or bad. Everything is not visible, and things are not always as they seem to us from outside another's situation.

THOUGHT 7: GET A GRIP ON YOUR FEARS

We have a love/hate thing with fear. We love healthy fears because they can serve us in certain ways, like when we look both ways before crossing the street so we don't get hit by a bus. We hate fear, too, because it makes us feel uncomfortable, distracted, and really stressed (such as the fear of losing a job, a relationship, or money). It robs us of enjoying the present and the things we do have.

Fear can be so paralyzing that we don't do anything, thinking we might make a situation worse or so all-consuming that it causes us to make poor decisions – decisions that are about avoiding more pain as opposed to seeking something better.

Sometimes we even inflict punishment on what we determine is causing us fear – fear which we cleverly try to disguise as anger (I say "disguise" because anger has its roots in fear). We get angry with someone or at some injustice waged upon us, then decide an appropriate and reasonable response is payback or punishment. Usually nobody wins and everyone loses with this strategy – not a very mature, enlightened, or productive response.

The capability to stop fearing something is probably one of the biggest issues of mankind. We all fear to some degree – most of the same things, too: loss, not having enough of what we think we need, not being good enough, being alone… actually, just about everything fits into the category of not having enough of what we think we need.

One way we can keep our fears on a tight leash is by reframing them from something we think requires fight (resistance and possibly counter-attack) or flight (avoidance, denial, giving up) to thoughts and responses that produce more desirable or preferred outcomes.

Let's say you know you're about to lose your job. Instead of squandering your energy on fearful thoughts and imagined scenarios, you can investigate your thoughts about what that actually means. Try to distinguish between the facts (loss of job, loss of income, etc.) and your fears (I'm not good enough, I have no value, I'm never going to find another job, I'm going to lose everything, etc.). Instead of using up your focus and energy on being afraid and letting your fears get completely out of control, use them to see what the truth of the situation is (I need to replace my income), and then focus on ways to do what you need to do. Practice managing your emotions (fear, anger, disappointment) by managing your thoughts, and practice managing your thoughts by specifically directing them to the facts and the task at hand. Keeping the emotion of fear in check allows you to think more clearly and rationally and decide on the right action to take.

We can choose to reframe the entire way we view a situation, move away from the thoughts that are holding us in the tight grip of fear, and step into the embrace of possibility – the idea that something good could come of the situation. We can have faith that it's time for our next growth spurt, and though that often means enduring some growing pains, if we set our sights on the potential good we can come through the scary and uncomfortable phase as transformed people.

Another biggie is learning how to stop fearing what we *imagine* is going to happen. A tough one, I know. Sometimes we're actually afraid to stop being afraid! We mistakenly think that if we don't fear something it might mean (or appear to others) that we don't care about it or are minimizing its importance. But we can still care or have concerns about something without fearing it. How many times have you been afraid of something looming ahead and it either never happens or is much less awful than you thought it was going to be? Or maybe the worst did happen, but you ultimately evolved to a better place as a result.

Let's say you decide to live in Tornado Alley:

Is it wise to be concerned that a tornado could come along and wipe out your house? Of course.

Do you know beyond the shadow of a doubt that this absolutely will happen? No.

Should you take every precaution and be as prepared as possible so that if it does happen you have a plan in place to deal with it? Yes.

Other than moving, is there anything else you can do? No.

Oh wait, there is one more thing you can do: Live in fear. You can be terrified every single day that a tornado will come along and wipe out your house. You can be afraid to plant a garden, to picnic in the yard, to add on an addition, to let the kids swing. You can squander the opportunity to be happy and enjoy what you have now because a tornado might come along someday in the future.

The better way to think about it is:

If a tornado is going to happen, it will. And you will have done all you could to deal with it.

If a tornado is not going to happen, it won't. And you will have done all you could, just in case.

How does living in fear and being terrified every day of what may or may not happen help anything or serve anyone? Does the fear promote or prevent the tornado? What if it never happens? Or let's say it does happen. Let's say you live in Tornado Alley for ten years and then a tornado comes and wipes out your house. Would you want to have spent the ten tornado-free years enjoying your life or miserable with fear? The ten years is going to pass whether a tornado comes along or not. The question is, in what state of mind do you want to spend those ten years?

THOUGHT 8: ACCEPT WHERE YOU ARE

Next practice ACCEPTING WHERE YOU ARE. Know that you are on the path you are supposed to be on. How do you know? Because that's where you are. If you were supposed to be somewhere else you would be. Appreciate where you are on your path right now. If it's not a place you feel you should be then you are resisting what IS, also known as REALITY, and causing yourself stress and frustration. Did you catch that? I'll repeat it just to be sure. CAUSING YOURSELF STRESS AND FRUSTRATION. Embracing the fact that you are the biggest cause of your stress gives you the control to make changes.

Things only suck when we decide they suck and then wallow in it. If you decide that something in your life sucks, then fine – so you say to yourself, "Ok, this sucks. I don't like this, and I prefer something different now." Learn something from the situation and prepare to make changes. The changes need to be directed at yourself and your own circumstances, not at other people and circumstances that you can't control.

It's simply less stressful and more fun to enact change coming from a place of emotional peace, clear thinking, responsibility, and acceptance rather than one of anger, resistance, or resentment. Acceptance does not mean giving up or giving in. It means not resisting what currently IS – because it already IS. Not accepting what IS doesn't change what IS, it just makes you miserable (and probably those around you who have to listen to you whine and complain about it). Acceptance helps you stabilize your emotions, and stable emotions let you think more clearly.

Then there's gratitude. Stop and think about what you might be grateful for, especially in the most uncomfortable of situations. There's always something to be grateful for, and if you can't find anything you're either not looking hard enough or you're really comfortable playing the victim. Hopefully you can be honest enough with yourself to take responsibility for your part in your circumstances. Learn from those circumstances and forget about criticizing yourself and beating yourself up about them. The opportunity for growth and the freedom to make changes – now those are gifts to be grateful for.

NOW ACT! Make your changes! It's perfectly okay to prefer something different. New choices and actions can save your life! You have the freedom to make new choices, and now you can make them from a place of appreciation, clear thinking, and calm intention.

THOUGHT 9: TAKE RESPONSIBILITY

Take responsibility for your happiness. There are ways we shirk the responsibility for nurturing our own happiness that aren't always so obvious. Do you divert energy and focus from your own growth and fulfillment so you can spend it on others? Do you think to yourself, "I don't have time to focus on my needs and what makes me happy because I have kids and they always come first," or "I have a job and too many other responsibilities to focus on my own health and well-being"? Or maybe you've heard this one: "How can I be happy when my job/my partner/my health/this situation is making me miserable?"

…A lot of questions, I know, but asking yourself the hard questions is often what makes you stop and think deeply enough about something to truly gain some insight and clarity. Being comfortable with excuses like the ones above will make it almost impossible to achieve the results that you desire – if your desire is to be truly happy and fulfilled. If you never take responsibility and make time to cultivate a happier life, how will you have one?

It's up to us to shift the balance. Naturally we need to direct focus and energy toward our kids, spouses, partners, responsibilities, etc., and it's essential to our fulfillment that we do so and that we try our best to fill the needs of those we care about. When that balance gets so lopsided that it's at the expense of our own well-being, and there are negative physical, spiritual, and emotional effects, we need to re-evaluate and see if we are due for an adjustment in how we are prioritizing our energy and focus.

When we own the responsibility for our happiness, we're usually better parents, better employees, better bosses, better friends, better lovers, and better at handling our obligations (which naturally results in more happiness!).

THOUGHT 10: THE CONTINGENCY PLAN

By neglecting the nourishment of your own well-being (growth, health, the pursuit of happiness), you deprive yourself and others of the best of YOU. This doesn't mean you should neglect your responsibilities or curb your support of those you love and care for; it means don't neglect yourself. Care for yourself, too. You need to GROW, too! You want to be a strong, self-fulfilling individual who is able to share your happiness, your life, your experiences, and your best self with others – without a contingency plan. You know, the plan that goes something like this: "I'll be good only if you'll be good," "I'll give my best only if you give yours," "I'll love you unconditionally only if you'll love me back unconditionally," (that's a good one – a condition on being willing to love unconditionally) "I'll behave with integrity only if you do," "If you're not an ass to me, I won't be an even bigger ass to you," "I'll do the right thing if everyone else does." Get it? Sounds pretty selfish and childish when you put it like that doesn't it?

What kind of person have you decided to be? What are your standards? How important is it to you to live up to your standards? Is acting with integrity something you value?

You can give and share even when others are not willing to do so. That's where the joy is – in the giving and sharing – and you can experience that joy even if those things are not returned if that's the kind of person you've decided to be. You can be willing to give and share and maintain your integrity by holding yourself to that standard regardless of outcomes or others' behavior, or you can lower your standards and allow your integrity to be compromised when you don't get the response you want or expect. Integrity isn't living by the rules and standards that other people have set; it's being true to the rules and standards that you set for yourself.

Can you maintain your integrity and hold to your standards because that's what you believe is right? Can you do it even when no one is watching or when someone else angers or disappoints you? Do you have the courage to remain true to yourself and to the standards you've set for yourself? Can you do what you believe is right even when it's really uncomfortable?

When I was about five years old, I was playing with a little girl at the house of a friend of my mom's. Every time I picked up a toy to play with she would grab it out of my hands. I'd let her have it and look for something else, but no matter which toy I picked, she wanted it – or rather she didn't want me to have it. I was baffled. Her strange behavior didn't make me want to mimic her, barter with her (if you give me your toy I'll give you mine), or start grabbing toys out of her hands – I just thought she was nutty. I told my mom about it later and she said that was called being selfish. Aha! There was a name for that unattractive behavior. Her selfishness and unwillingness to share didn't make me want to be selfish back; it made me see that it was something I didn't want to be.

It's really a shame to stop giving your gifts of love, respect, forgiveness, empathy, or acts of sharing with others simply because they haven't learned to do so. Don't be stingy with your gifts. Be generous.

What you practice thinking, doing, and being over and over again is what shows up as your experience – what creates your life maze. So consciously decide what kind of person you want to be and BE it. Refrain from mirroring others' bad behavior, and don't lower your integrity by lowering the bar just because others do. You be the best self you know how to be – that's your business. How others decide to be is their business. If you want to have a calm and harmonious approach to life, then do – even if those around you are screaming and creating chaos. If you want to experience understanding and compassion, then be understanding and compassionate – even when others are not. If you want joy and humor in your life, then be joyful and laugh with others, laugh at yourself, and laugh in the face of adversity, too. If you want to feel bad and miserable, you will. If you don't, you won't.

Decide what standards and values are right for you and then hold yourself responsible for living them.

THOUGHT 11: JUST KISS

We tend to over-complicate things and come up with all sorts of reasons – based on our past experiences or imagined futures – to justify feeling the way we feel and acting the way we act. When it comes to owning your happiness, I find the "Just K.I.S.S." method works pretty well for me: "Just keep it super simple." (I know the popular saying is "Keep it simple stupid," but that just seems so rude, and I don't want anyone to take it personally and feel insulted! Besides, most of us aren't stupid; we just do stupid things sometimes. Big difference.)

There are times when you have to pause and take a very deep breath and just break life down to one moment at a time – the present moment, then the next present moment, then the next… and in each of those moments remember to CHOOSE. Choose to be that which makes you feel good about who you are and demonstrates the greater version of yourself that you are striving to become. Choose to be that person who rises above, who can give more, understand more, and love more.

It's so hard to see the simplicity of how to move forward when you complicate your life with stuff that shouldn't matter, no longer matters, or doesn't even exist yet! It's like shadow boxing – swinging at something that's not really there. What a waste of energy!

I know it's not always easy to make new choices, to rise above, to be more. We've all said and done things at one time or another that we've regretted and known was not within our standards of integrity, either because we were still learning what kind of person we wanted to be or because we just let ourselves get caught in the current of the drama at hand. We know when it happens, too, because we don't feel good about ourselves afterwards. That feeling of guilt, regret, or uneasiness we get is our internal guide telling us something. Listen to it, learn, and keep practicing who and how you want to BE.

THOUGHT 12: WHO'S IN CHARGE HERE?

I don't think we're here to be sculpted and molded by others. Isn't that what we're inadvertently doing when we live in a reactive state – when we do and say things in reaction to what others do and say? I don't believe that God, Mother Nature, the Life Force, or the Universe (pick whatever reference works for you) makes mistakes. I think we are here to live our lives fully by expressing and creating in our own ways that which brings us – and others – joy.

Once we are no longer dependent upon our parents, we are meant to make our own choices; hopefully ones that will lead us to be happy, positive, contributing members of society – indeed, of the human race. Don't place the course of your life in the hands of others and shirk responsibility for your contentment. That job is meant for you. You have dominion over your own body, mind, and spirit. Those three things comprise your present experience of YOU. Why would you entrust your well-being of YOU and your expression of being truly YOU to anyone other than, well, YOU? Take charge of your life maze!

Remember, the experience of your life is temporary, and most of us have no earthly idea just how temporary it's going to be. The only real certainty is that it's temporary. Reminding yourself of that can be a powerful motivator for not squandering your life on stupid crap like holding grudges, creating or adding to drama, or just overall being a negative cloud of energy when it's really so unnecessary. Being super-cognizant of what's right in front of you – of where you are, what you are saying and thinking, and who you are demonstrating yourself to be – is really quite powerful. Behaving in reaction to what others around you are doing and saying and allowing yourself to be moved from your place of integrity is letting others make you dance like a puppet on a string.

My husband has spent the better part of the last twenty years traveling, as was required by his profession. So I spent lots and lots of time alone and taking care of our two children by myself. Many times over the years people asked me, "How can you stand being alone so much?" or commented, "That must be so hard; I could never do it." And others in the same situation told me they hated it. Of course I missed my husband when he was gone, and I know he missed me and our kids, but while he was busy working and creating, so was I. I wasn't just going through the motions until he came home to make me happy and fulfilled; I learned to do that myself. I did my part of our responsibilities with love, enthusiasm, and passion, including taking care of our children, our family affairs, and ME! Sure there were some times when I wished he were around to help chauffer the kids all over town or deal with a leaky roof, but I know he also had thoughts like, "Man, I wish I were at home with my wife and kids right now instead of getting on another plane. I wish I could just play hooky this week and stay home and eat dinner in my own kitchen with my family."

The point is we decided what would work for us, made our choices, and approached our tasks and life together as teammates. We each took responsibility for our roles as we defined them together. I wanted to do my job as best I could, and I also wanted to be my best "self." Tending to my health and well-being is what enabled me to approach even the mundane chores of daily living with a sense of pride and joy. I figured out that when you don't short-change yourself, you don't feel so resentful about doing the not-so-fun stuff. The more I took charge of nurturing and taking care of me, which meant staying balanced between being a good mom, a good wife, and good to myself, the more I felt fulfilled as an individual and in control of my happiness and level of contentment.

THOUGHT 13: NURTURE YOURSELF

How do you nurture yourself? It varies from person to person, but for me it meant nourishing my mind, my body, and my spirit. I nourished my mind by continuing to learn. I didn't want to spend time away from my family going to classes, so I read about whatever I wanted to learn about such as nutrition, fitness, parenting, politics, spirituality, personal growth, the classics – whatever, I read about it. I read a little bit when the kids were in school and I read after they went to bed. I nourished my body by making exercise a regular part of my life and educated myself about food and nutrition.

Tending to your physical well-being reaps not only the obvious benefits of maintaining good health, but does wonders for your sense of confidence and inner happiness. If you're a parent, it also demonstrates to your kids that you place a high value on taking care of yourself, and they will see that as the norm.

Then there's the spirit part. That's your own personal deal. For me it has always been and still is family time and reading spiritual and inspirational books. I can pick up a book that speaks to me and get my spiritual fix any time I want without having to leave my house or adjust my schedule to anyone else's. I can "go to church" by connecting with the Universe/God several times a day through my thoughts, awareness and meditation. I also feel very spiritually connected when I'm doing just about anything outside. As I've gotten older and evolved, many of my most spiritually nourishing things experiences are when I'm contributing beyond myself. Coaching and helping others really does that for me.

If going to church is important to you, then you should go. If you get a spiritual shot in the arm by just being out in nature, then carve out time to do that. Whatever it is that gives you that sense of joy – like you're just totally lined up with something – some larger-than-life mystery vibe that you may not even be able to describe – that, to me, is church. Might be that you get that from painting, horseback riding, wood working, dancing, donating your services, or any one of an infinite list of things. Simply expressing your natural talent can facilitate harmony and joy and be spiritual – a way to tap in to and connect with the magic of life.

I really enjoyed taking care of our home and affairs. I looked forward to seeing my husband every time he came home, not because I needed him to take care of me or entertain me, but because he is the man I love and I couldn't wait to catch up, share our experiences, and enjoy each other and the life we were creating together. Can you imagine how he would have felt if after having been gone for days – doing the airport thing, living out of a suitcase, working his ass off and missing his home and family – he would have come home and been greeted with, "Good, you're finally back. Now make me happy, make me whole, entertain me. I'm so lonely and bored without you." Or what if he would have had the same expectations of me? Geez, what a burden! He looked forward to coming home to someone who was able to sustain herself and didn't have needy expectations. Because we owned the responsibility for making ourselves happy, we were happy. We were working as a team, each creating our individual mazes, while simultaneously giving our best to each other and nurturing our family maze – a result of our individual mazes connecting and intertwining.

THOUGHT 14: BIG FAT GLITCHES

Happiness is a state of being that must be cultivated from within. That also makes it your choice. You can't expect to live in a state of happiness if you keep looking for it to be delivered from other people, stuff, events, money, etc. All those things can definitely be loved and enjoyed, but if your happiness is based on your attachment to them, what will happen if or when they're no longer there? What if something or someone doesn't meet your expectations or love you back? What if a big fat glitch in your plan happens? Can you still be happy?

I mean let's face it; we can't control every situation and person we encounter. Things will be as they will be and they will also change. But we can control our experience of them. It doesn't mean there won't be times when we feel sadness, frustration, and other difficult or unpleasant emotions, but we can try to use these feelings and situations to serve us and recognize that it's normal to feel unpleasant emotions now and then and to be okay until they subside. As we spoke about earlier, our emotions stem from our thoughts about things, and WE decide the meaning and value we apply to those things. For example, let's say it's snowing like crazy. One person may look outside and think, "Oh, crap. This is bad. This snow is really awful. Now I'm going to have to dig my car out, the roads will be terrible, and I'm going to be cold and miserable." Another person may see that it's snowing out and exclaim, "Yeah, it's finally snowing! This is awesome! Just what I've been waiting for! I'm going to have a blast today because I can finally go skiing!" The point is that snow is snow. It's white, wet, and cold. Period. Good, bad, awful, and awesome are judgments we make about the snow according to what we decide it's going to mean to us and how we want to feel about it. The same goes for people and happenings. They just are what they are. You decide what meanings to apply, and your thoughts and those meanings create your experience.

I know we've discussed this already, but I want to come at it again from a slightly different angle to make sure it hits home with you. If we agree that our emotions are actually a physical manifestation of our thoughts, we can understand that we own the power to make ourselves happy or miserable. We can say to ourselves, "Well, right now this sucks and I feel like crap, but I recognize that I'm choosing to feel this way, and I know I have the power to choose to feel another way when I'm ready to." Or, "I think I'll just decide to feel great regardless of the fact that so-and-so is acting like a complete jerk and taking out their frustrations on me. I'm not going to take it personally and give them the power to affect my mood."

THOUGHT 15: BE WHO YOU'RE LOOKING FOR

Be that which you would like to experience or see in others. I had a client who was working hard to find peace and harmony in her life. She had been in a very emotionally intense and resentful place for a long, long time. Her relationship with her husband was strained to the max. She had a strong personality and was quite accustomed to flying off the handle in angry outbursts. Her family tried to guess what would make her happy at any given moment and adapt their behavior accordingly, usually unsuccessfully. Ever known someone around whom you feel you always have to walk on eggshells lest you make the wrong step and all hell breaks loose? It's a terrible feeling and a horrible way to make others feel.

It's draining and miserable to live in constant fear that something you say or do is going to make the volcano erupt.

My client finally recognized that it was her behavior that was volatile and creating stress for her and everyone else. Finally one day during one of our sessions, she passionately exclaimed, "I just want peace!" I said, "Then BE peace." She paused, thought for a moment, and realized that the ball was in her court. No one was going to deliver a box of peace to her door. She could not enjoy peace if she kept creating chaos. When she was willing to broaden her perspective and take responsibility, she began to see that she was creating much of her undesirable situation and unhappiness herself. She realized that she had to start learning and practicing how to BE that which she desired to experience, and accept that she just might not be able to get what she wanted from her current situation. Once she finally accepted that the situation and the hubby might not ever change in the way she thought they should, she was able to understand that change was still possible – it just had to be on her end. She stopped resisting the current reality and started focusing on her own actions and choices. She started thinking about what *she* could do to begin cultivating peace and happiness.

If you want a partner who is self-sufficient, independent, happy, and gives their best to you and the relationship, you must endeavor to be and do those things, too. If you are a parent who wants those things for your children, show them what that looks like. If you want people in your life who possess those qualities – as they say, like attracts like.

THOUGHT 16: WHAT DO YOU WANT?

If you want a happier life, start thinking about what that would look and feel like to you. Think about what really makes you happy. There are a lot of people who know what they don't want but don't know what they do want. Obviously, at a minimum, we all want to have our basic needs met. But then there's all that other stuff we want. Just gotta have it! Why? There are reasons like: "It will make my life better. It will make me look better. It will solve my problems. It will make me more likeable, loveable, do-able. It/he/she will make me happy." The lines between need and want can become very, very gray. I won't try to tell you what should be in your need and want categories; I'm just saying that it's easy to overlook the good things in your life and the quality of how you live your life when you get too focused on what you think you have to acquire in order to be happier.

You can zero in on what you want by just paying attention! And it doesn't require a credit card! Noticing what's going on around you can be pretty fulfilling and entertaining. Have you ever just watched kids playing, people dancing, or your family just doing ordinary things? Don't you just want to laugh when you see someone else really laughing? (Careful, yawning is like that too.)

Think back to some good memories you have from your childhood. Are they about money or expensive things? Or are they about how you experienced something or someone that made you feel so good you still remember it to this day. I remember getting my first bike. Scared the heck out of me at first. Took me what seemed like forever to learn to ride the thing. My little sister learned to ride it before I did (damn her anyway!). But once I did, oh my, did I ride. I rode and rode. You see, it wasn't so much about the bike, or that I could get from point A to point B faster (although a nice perk), and it didn't matter to me how much it cost or that it wasn't the most expensive money could buy; It was about the freedom and the fun and the experience of the ride. I rode my bike until I learned to drive, and then that was that – until just recently. Thirty-some years after I stopped riding I got another bike and started riding again. After talking about it for a year, my husband and I finally decided to either start riding again or stop talking about it. So we bought bikes – beach cruisers to be exact.

When I got on my bike after all those years, I instantly felt like a kid again, just playing. That sense of fun and freedom filled me up as much as it had when I was a kid. I grinned like an idiot for an hour straight while I rode, re-living my youth. Actually, it was like getting a bonus round! My new bike cost less than a movie and a decent dinner out for two.

Quality is what I'm talking about here. Keep your eye on the target. Upping your happy meter may be less expensive and less complicated than you think!

SUMMARY, PRINCIPLE 1 – HAPPY: TO BE OR NOT TO BE

1. Take responsibility for your happiness.
2. Stop focusing on and judging others.
3. Accept where you are at this moment.
4. Act with clear intention.
5. Bring your happiness and completeness to the dance with you.

PRINCIPLE 2

hold your
POWER

"Have the courage to say no. Have the courage to face the truth. Do the right thing because it is right. These are the magic keys to living your life with integrity."
※ W. CLEMENT STONE ※

THOUGHT 1: "BUT YOU MADE ME FEEL..."

What does "Hold Your Power" mean? What is your "power?" It's not about pushing your desires onto others, but more about owning and standing strong in what's true for you. I think of it as embracing and practicing personal responsibility and control of our own thoughts, emotions, and actions, and using that skill to become all we desire for ourselves.

How many times have you found yourself upset by something someone else said to you or about you? Usually this is followed by a reactive emotion or behavior. When we allow someone else's words to affect us negatively, we give up our power. We just give it away. Why? We come up with all sorts of logical-sounding reasons, such as "I needed to defend myself," "I wasn't going to let them get away with that," "That person really put me in a bad mood," or "That person really made me angry." Most reasons reflect our need for others' approval or to feel right (superior) by making the other person feel wrong (inferior).

When you fall into the trap of feeling offended, insulted, belittled, or inspired to act out in a negative way as a result of someone else's words or behavior, you have effectively just given that person the keys to your emotions – your power. That's a helpless feeling and a bad habit. It can't possibly make you feel good, and most often makes you feel like crap. Don't become a prisoner – a slave to your emotions – by taking things others say or do so personally that you become trapped in an undesirable emotional state.

If someone came up to you and let out a tirade of insulting, hurtful, and offending words, but in a language you didn't understand, would their words have any real impact on you? Probably not. Most likely you would just think they were nuts, ignore them, and go about your business, because their words would only be sounds – sounds with absolutely no meaning to you and therefore ineffective in their ability to manipulate your emotions.

Words carelessly uttered by others really don't have any meaning other than the meaning you choose to give them. If someone's words aren't constructive and don't serve you well, don't get emotionally nauseous by eating them. Hold your power by refusing to ingest them in the first place. Pretend they're speaking Latin if you have to! I guarantee if you practice this you will experience a newfound sense of freedom. *You* are then the gatekeeper of your emotions and your self-worth, not someone else. Don't give them the keys!

A seemingly insignificant comment can have a large and lasting effect on a person. When I was about six years old, I was gazing in the mirror at myself. I remember the feeling of liking what I saw. As I was still fairly new in the world, I was enjoying becoming familiar with the little person my soul had chosen to inhabit. I was a happy kid and smiled at myself in the mirror. My dad walked by and asked, "What are you looking at?" with a bit of a snide attitude that let me know that he did not approve – that it was not okay for someone to gaze at themself in the mirror. Then I heard him ask my mother why I was staring at myself in the mirror. I do not recall her response, but I got the clear message that it was wrong, which made me feel confused and self-conscious. "Am I not supposed to like myself?" I wondered.

This was the first experience I can recall that made me feel like I wasn't free to be myself; I was made to feel guilty for liking myself. Of course as a child, I wasn't equipped with the insight to know that my dad's words didn't have to influence me, so naturally they did. And it wasn't really his intention to send the message that he sent. But a seed was planted. A natural response to that kind of message is to seek approval from others, since you no longer feel comfortable giving it to yourself – not the healthiest approach for developing self-confidence and discovering how to hold your power.

In later years I realized that my dad didn't really like himself all that much, so he inadvertently projected his feelings about self-esteem onto me. This was the first chipping away at my power that I recall experiencing. Many of us experience a stifling of our power as we grow up and, unfortunately, for some it is intense and has a lasting negative impact. I had a couple more such experiences with teachers. Geez, but some of them should get different careers! Fortunately my good teachers outweighed my not-so-good ones!

If you have a negative belief about yourself, it may have grown from a seed that was planted in you when you were a child by someone you looked up to or who had influence over you, like a parent, relative, or teacher. It's really important to investigate such beliefs and understand that just because you have them doesn't mean they're true. Someone may have lied to you. It may have been unintentional, but the result is the same: your feelings of self-worth and the way you respond to people and situations are coming from a mind-set that's holding a false belief. You can undo the effects of your false beliefs by closely analyzing them and refusing to let them influence you any longer for no good reason.

I have long since reclaimed my power. I know now that it's not only okay to like and actually love yourself, but it's also healthy and necessary in order to be really happy, to accept others as they are, and to be able to love unconditionally.

This doesn't mean you should turn a deaf ear to someone who has something to say to you that you don't like. There can be truth in the words of others that is uncomfortable to hear. But if you don't let your pride and ego get in your way, those same words could be constructive and help you see something in yourself that you may want to work on.

THOUGHT 2: OWN IT OR BE OWNED

Practice holding your power by not giving it away to other people or activities that make you feel like less than who you are. Figure out the qualities and characteristics that you value, and then live them. Your power comes from learning what values you hold dear, what kind of a person you do and don't want to be, and treating yourself and others with integrity. Don't compromise your values to blend in with the crowd or meet others' approval. If you allow someone else to talk you into doing something that in your heart you really don't want to do, you've given that person your power. If you agree with someone else about something that you actually strongly disagree with because you think that person will like you more, you've betrayed your power. If you engage in nasty gossip about another, you've abused your power. If you make a habit of over-indulging in unhealthy quantities of food, alcohol, or harmful substances, you've diminished and sabotaged your power. Make sense?

If you don't own your power, it's easy for other people and things to OWN YOU. Those people and things can now create or greatly influence the maze of your life. You are effectively letting them establish the parameters of your life – whether you will turn right or left or just wander in circles – causing confusion and making it difficult to get closer to your desired destination and live as your true self. You may or may not have figured out what you want to be when you grow up, or what you want to do next in life, or exactly where you want to go, but you can still own how you want to *be* in this world and *how* you want to travel and evolve. That's holding your power.

THOUGHT 3: ENERGY THIEVES

Another way we can hold our power is to not let "energy thieves" – aka "energy vampires" or "energy vacuums" – steal it. Energy thieves are like vacuums – they consume all the energy around them to fuel and nourish themselves. Have you ever spent time around someone and felt drained afterward? They're like low batteries and you're the battery charger. They sense (usually subconsciously) a source of positive energy, hook up to you, and proceed to suck the life out of you.

Moms in particular know exactly what I'm talking about. A mom often becomes the battery charger for the rest of the family, as her natural tendency is to be the caretaker and give to everyone else 24/7 without boundaries or opportunities to recharge herself. Not to say that our little ones are energy vampires;

let's refer to them as energy angels. They require a great deal of our energy, and as parents we are responsible for their care. If you're a parent, just be aware that you need to recharge your battery frequently to protect yourself from becoming completely drained.

When it comes to people who are not under your care, however, it pays to be cautious and protect yourself. I'm not talking about isolated situations in which you need to be there for someone going through a rough patch. I'm talking about people for whom this is their way of being, all the time – the person who always talks non-stop, constantly demanding all of your attention, talking at you instead of with you. They are only interested in having you hear them, not in your input (unless it's sympathetic). Their conversation is autobiographical as opposed to empathetic; they always bring the conversation around to themselves, their own experiences, and their own opinions. If you begin to relay a story about a personal experience, rather than just listening or asking you to elaborate they interrupt you to talk about their own related story, and then don't even have the interest to come back to yours.

Energy thieves are often "drama queens," always insisting on making a big deal out of the littlest thing, going on and on and on about it. Energy thieves are self-absorbed, tend to complain and vent, and are generally unconcerned about or unaware of their effect on you. They just seem to have a voracious appetite for attention! You can recognize an energy thief by the way you feel after you've spent time in their company. If you notice a pattern of feeling drained, annoyed, or exhausted, they have been stealing your energy! But if you feel like you come away with a sense of enjoyment from someone – a feeling of being uplifted, or like you were on the same page with them – then you know that they were not stealing energy from you. Make sure you return the gift.

Understanding and identifying energy thieves doesn't mean you can't live with, spend time with, or have a relationship with them. It doesn't mean they're evil, deliberately trying to steal your energy, or on a mission to destroy you. They are just seeking positive energy to fill something in them that you may not understand.

There may be many people in your life whom you love and enjoy very much, but who are energy thieves. You just need to learn how to avoid being drained by them! Recognize it first; then you can still enjoy them but protect yourself at the same time by managing your expectations, limiting your time with them (when possible), staying somewhat detached in conversations with them, avoiding getting sucked into their negativity, and maintaining your boundaries.

If you know you're going to be around someone who typically likes to do all the talking, your goal should be to just listen. Unless they're on fire and don't know it, don't try to force yourself into their conversation, other than to acknowledge what they're saying. Give them the gift of listening to them – with boundaries. When you feel your gift is turning into a major chore and starting to drain you, you're done. Politely and subtly remove yourself from the situation.

You may need to limit your contact with such a person (or group) to situations that you can control and get away from easily and tactfully. If you're going to a social gathering where there will be energy thieves, don't become a prisoner by traveling with the pack; drive there yourself so you can make your exit when you know your fun meter has peaked. Remove yourself while you still feel good about everyone, before you become annoyed or drained.

THOUGHT 4: WALK THE PLANK!

Find out what you're really capable of. Every now and then we need to do something we either always wanted to do or never thought we'd do – something that's outside our typical box. New worlds can open up for you if you're brave enough (or crazy enough) to just take a flying leap every once in a while. Let me tell you about a flying leap I took – literally.

I had made up my mind a while back that one day I was going to take a flying trapeze lesson. So "one day" came and I really committed. I decided to make it part of an intensive coaching session that I had planned with mother-daughter clients of mine. I told them that I would be participating in the lesson with them. After all, how could I expect them to try something I was not willing to try myself?

The physically uncomfortable feeling I get when I'm up high is rather annoying. I have to breathe deeply, steel my nerves, and remind myself that logically I'm perfectly safe – even though it doesn't feel that way and my body wants to argue otherwise. My daughter told me I have a fear of heights. I said, "No, I don't. I'm not actually afraid of heights; my body just doesn't like them!" She said, "Yeah, that's called a fear of heights."

I still disagree.

When I told my clients what I had in store, I also revealed to them that I have just a teeny bit of a hard time with heights. I think they felt better – like they wouldn't be walking the plank alone.

So the three of us went trembling, yet boldly, where none of us had gone before. After listening to the initial spiel from the instructors about what to expect and what the rules were, and after a few minutes of warm-up practice positions, they said, "Okay, who's up first?" One guess as to who that was.

Up the very steep and skinny ladder I nervously crawled to what appeared to be a postage-stamp-sized platform from which I would plunge to my new confidence level. I was shaking with fear and forcing myself not to look down. From below it didn't seem terribly high, and relatively speaking, it wasn't. But standing up on the narrow platform looking down, it seemed extreme-sport high.

I did what the instructor told me to and stepped to the edge of the platform and wrapped my toes over it. My left hand still gripped the rail, anchored to the platform, while my right hand reached out to grab the swing he was pulling toward me.

At this point I was leaning out over the edge so far that my weight would have pulled my body right off the platform had the instructor not been holding the safety belt on my waist, which is exactly how he said things were supposed to be. Then I was told to let go of the rail I was tightly gripping with my left hand, reach out, and grab the other side of the swing that my right hand was already holding.

Seriously? If I do that, I'm thinking, then I have to trust that he will continue to hold me and keep me from plunging headfirst over the edge. This instruction went quite counter to my instinct – you know, that survival one. Every reflex in my body was telling me I was in a dangerously precarious position and that continuing on this path could not possibly be in my best interest.

And yet there I was, dangling by my temporary insanity, and being held in place by some beach dude with a cowboy hat strapped to his chin whom I had just met minutes earlier.

But I'm a good student, and I needed to demonstrate that I was a courageous and fearless leader in front of my clients, who were pensively peering up at me from six miles below. So I did as I was instructed. I took a deep breath – actually several of them – and grabbed the bar with my other hand. Oh God, oh God, oh God, this was scary shit! Even with safety cables, nets, and a beachcowboy-trapeze-guy wrangling me through the process! It was time. He told me to bend my knees slightly and then…

I flew. Off the platform, out over the net, just holding on to the bar with my own two hands, and I was swinging through the air over the Santa Monica Pier. Whoa.

It was fun for like a second, because just as I was getting somewhat comfortable with that move and beginning to rejoice in the fact that I wasn't sprawled unladylike on the net far beneath me, the next instruction echoed its way up to me from far below: "Now bring your feet up and over the bar – bar – bar!"

Sure. "Abs, if you're in there somewhere, now's a good time to come out and join in the fun" was my next thought/prayer/plea. I had to jolt them into action, but they came through. Thank you, God of the Bod. Now I'm thinking, "I got this! I'm hanging upside down and all is well. Not too bad!" The next instruction was yelled up: "Now let go of the bar with your hands." "Hmm," I briefly pondered, "let's see. When I let go with my hands I will then be swinging upside down by my knees – and only my knees." I hesitated, but only for a moment. At this point I was not feeling like I had much negotiating power, so I let go of the bar, and voilà! Much to my surprise I was still on the swing! Whew!

"Okay now as you swing back, arch and reach out behind you toward the sky!" I was feeling quite graceful and almost Cirque du Soleil material as I glided through the air. "All righty then! I got this!" It actually felt really good. Finally I was told to reach back up and grab the bar, unhook my legs, look up toward the sky, and let go of the bar. Supposedly you're then to land gracefully on your back in the net. Somehow – I couldn't tell you why – I landed on my face. I was just fine with that.

My clients and I repeated this same routine several times and then we were ready for part two. Part two? I didn't recall reading about that.

Part two: All was the same as part one, except that once I was upside down, flying through the air, swinging by my legs, I was supposed to arch, reach back, and grab the ever-so-capable gentleman who had magically appeared on the opposite side swinging upside down by his legs on the opposite side. Where the hell did he come from?

At this point, still shaking, I thought, "Why not? Can it get much scarier?" I crawled up the ladder again, assumed the position with the guidance of my new BFF-beachcowboy-trapeze-guy, and leaped. I went through the routine, feeling pretty okay with it by now, and then came the part where I was upside down and was supposed to reach.

This one action, which seemed like the one to fear the most, turned out, much to my surprise and delight, to be the least scary and the most amazing one of all. With my arms outstretched, I looked for my swinging-upside-down-ever-so-capable-gentleman-rescuer, and bada-bing – like God, he was already there, just waiting for me to show up. He grabbed my arms and said, "I gotcha." In that moment those were the two most magical words I'd ever heard. He was instantly promoted from gentleman-rescuer to my freakin' hero category. And just like that, part two was accomplished. Easy peasy.

With great trust in me and in my intentions, as well as in the fantastic instructors at the trapeze school (TSNY, Los Angeles), my clients proceeded to do something they had never even dreamed of doing, and I had done something I had. And what did we all get?

Uniquely empowered. We all went through the same physical motions but we each took different things away from the experience – things that will serve each of us in our own personal growth.

My "mom" client was navigating the road through a divorce at the time, was afraid of losing her relationships with her children, and had almost zero confidence that she could take care of herself. She also thought that at age fifty her best days were behind her. Fear of loss had become her full-time companion. After our lesson, she said that beforehand she had thought she was too old to do something like that and would never even have considered it. It gave her a new outlook on what she was capable of and could still do. The concept of possibilities started to creep back into her awareness. She was also happy to have been able to share the experience with her daughter. It was great to see them talking about it and laughing together. Her daughter exclaimed loudly as we were leaving the pier, "Now I feel like I can do anything!" What more could you want a fifteen-year-old to feel like? Mission accomplished.

I asked my clients to trust me – to do something they had never done and were nervous about. I asked them to literally take a leap of faith and believe that no matter what, they would be fine – and just maybe even better than fine.

I had to do the same exact thing. Not only did I have to trust someone else – the instructors – I also had to trust my initial impulse to try this stunt! I had to trust that there was a reason I was drawn to do this, and that if I followed through I would somehow be just a little bit better version of myself afterward.

In order to finish what I started, I really had to practice controlling my thoughts, which I knew would determine how I would feel and what I would do. I had to keep my thoughts on the facts and off my fear. Facts: The worst thing that could happen was that I would fall into a net, and the odds were excellent that I wouldn't die. The best thing that could happen was that I would have an amazing and wildly fun experience. Either way, I was going to end up in that net, crawl out, stand up, and decide what my next move would be. So I chose not to let my fear run the show and walk away – not to give up my power by giving in to my fear.

We are capable of much more than we realize. How will we know that, though, if we don't walk off the end of a plank once in a while? Each time we do, we have the opportunity to realize more of our potential and become more confident, more capable, and more adept at harnessing and holding our power. We learn that usually the worst that can happen often doesn't, and that if it does, we possess the strength and chutzpa to deal with it. Sometimes the worst that can happen is not allowing yourself to risk falling.

SUMMARY, PRINCIPLE 2 – HOLD YOUR POWER

1. Embrace and practice personal responsibility and control of you thoughts, emotions, and actions.

2. Don't take everything people say personally, but do be open to kernels of truth that may help you grow.

3. Protect your boundaries.

4. Take a flying leap once in a while.

make shift
HAPPEN

"Being happy doesn't mean that everything is perfect. It means that you've decided to look beyond the imperfections."
✦ FRIEDRICH NIETZSCHE ✦

THOUGHT 1: OH, SHIFT

When we're at our home in Wyoming, each morning I stand at the windows looking for the deer. There are deer living all around our house, and even though I've seen thousands of them over the years, I never get tired of it. I feel like it's a little present from nature every single time they appear. I can't tell you how many times I've stood at the window looking out over the hills for them and, not seeing them, started to turn away. But then something happens. Just as I shift and start to turn, I catch a glimpse of something. I refocus from my shifted position and there they are, right in front of me. They were standing or lying there all along, so close to me that I didn't even notice them. I was too busy searching for them in the distance. I've come to use this as a reminder that often what we are looking for is much closer than we realize. If we just shift our perspective and reel it in, even just a little, we can see it, right there in front of us, waiting to be noticed.

Then there are times we get so used to seeing everything from within the maze we've created that we can no longer see the forest for the trees. We can't see that there's something beyond what's right in front of us. We keep seeing things from the same limited perspective and don't realize that we keep traveling in the same circle. Then we wonder why the view – the situations and people around us – never changes. Or we think that what we need or want is not within our reach, that it's always somewhere else, or out there in the future. It's easy to get stuck looking at everyone and every situation from the narrow viewpoint of our maze. This is when we need to shift to a broader perspective.

THOUGHT 2: GET A BIRD'S-EYE VIEW

A new vantage point is a helpful tool for getting yourself unstuck – for breaking a pattern of limited and repetitive mindsets. I like visualization exercises. Here's one I sometimes use when I feel stuck, when I'm in a situation that seems to be getting the best of me, when I just can't see a solution, or even simply to contemplate stuff. I visualize myself rising up and out of my maze and sitting on the moon. It's quiet. It's calm. There are no competing energies. It's completely neutral. From this calm, neutral place, the noise and interference going on around me or even in my own head ceases to pull me in different directions away from my center and off balance. From this elevated position I can stabilize, get a fresh look at the bigger picture, and adjust my perspective on what's going on with me and around me. It also has the added benefit of making what appear to be huge obstacles or problematic situations seem much smaller – sometimes even downright insignificant. I often end up noticing that, like the deer, what I'm looking for is right in front of me. This visualization is often less about finding an answer or a solution than about finding a new attitude. You may prefer to visualize sitting on a mountaintop or floating in a hot air balloon – whatever resonates with you – just as long as it elevates you out of your maze so you can see things from a higher vantage point.

THOUGHT 3: MIND YOUR BUSINESS

You can also use this visualization technique to analyze how you got to where you are in your life right now. Shining a spotlight on the things we continue doing that keep us going in the same emotional circles – or as I so eloquently put it to my clients, swirling in a toilet bowl – helps us see what we need to change so we can start on a fresh path and stay out of the toilet bowl! But remember to keep your focus on *your* business, *your* actions, and *your* choices. Refrain from letting your mind wander to what others did or are doing.

As you gaze down upon your life from this elevated perspective, ask yourself, and try to honestly answer, the following how-was-my-life-maze-created questions (visit www.loreebischoff.com for a worksheet):

1. What parts of my life maze have I consciously created? (Intention)

2. What parts have I created unconsciously? (Not paying attention)

3. What parts seem to have been created for me? (You think someone else created them)

4. What parts were created out of reactive behavior? (You think, "I had to do that because X left me no choice.")

Ponder these questions deeply and try to answer them truthfully – *really* truthfully. Embrace the parts of your maze that are good, but also own up to your participation in the not-so-pleasant parts. If you can be brutally honest with yourself about the choices and decisions *you* made, even if you didn't realize you were making them at the time, you can start to see how your patterns, choices, and decisions have contributed to where you are now. Once you can accept what you are responsible for, it's pretty empowering, because you come to understand that if you are capable of creating stuff you aren't happy about, then you must be capable of creating stuff you can be happy about. This self-analyzing can help develop your power and your awareness of the choices and decisions you will continue to make as you endeavor to change or improve your life maze.

Not too long ago my business partner and I were planning a weekend-long life-coaching and motivational event for mothers, complete with well-known speakers and interactive workshops – the whole nine yards. My partner and I spent about eighteen months developing and planning this event. About half-way into the planning we teamed up with Person X who was to work on some very critical aspects of the marketing. It seemed that as each day went by and we got closer and closer to the big weekend, my frustration with this person grew and grew. Things weren't getting done as fast as we wanted or needed. There would be days and days when we couldn't reach Person X. Things we were led to believe would be executed were not. My patience (of which I have almost a bottomless pit) was absolutely exhausted. I felt somewhat deceived and really let down. I was afraid we wouldn't have the turnout we hoped for, and that part of the reason was that Person X was not making our vision a reality. I was so stressed I couldn't eat or sleep. I was on an emotional rollercoaster – alternately rising and plummeting between excitement and anticipation, stress and misery – at a time when I just wanted to enjoy creating something amazing to share.

Finally I just decided, "Enough already. What will be will be. The train has left the station. We will do the best we can and that's all we can do." So that's exactly what we did. Once the event was over I realized I needed to come to terms with the whole shebang. I didn't want the successful aspects of the event to be spoiled by those that had fallen short, or to be plagued with lingering, disappointing thoughts and resentment toward Person X. I did not want to be bitter or carry a big fat bag filled with grudges, blame, and other negative emotions. Feeling like that is burdensome, unproductive, and energy-draining, and is usually based on untruths or a warped, one-sided perspective of the situation. I knew enough to realize that there was a gift in there somewhere – a truth that would set my pissed-off mind free. And damn, but I needed to find it!

So I sat. I thought. I got a horrifically bad cold which forced me to do nothing but sit and think even more (and watch a weekend marathon of Dead-liest Catch). I meditated – a little. I talked it over and over with my partner. I thought more. I went to the moon, looked down, and saw the big picture. Aha! There it was – right in front of me. In fact, it *was* me. *I* was responsible. Ugh! But the facts are the facts, no matter how you decide to feel about them. Facts speak for themselves.

Fact: I made the choice to work with Person X. (How-was-my-life-maze-created Question #1 – Intention)

Fact: I chose to rely on someone else to do something without all the tools they needed. (Question #2 – Not paying attention to what could realistically be accomplished)

Fact: I chose to continue to work with Person X even when I wanted to pull my hair (and theirs) out because they were doing a less-than-successful job! (Question #3 – Someone else did it)

Fact: There was only x amount of money available in the budget I had to work with, but I chose to move forward anyway. (Question #4 – I had no choice)

I could go on, but you get the point.

So there was my gift. I had found it. Ahhh, freedom at last – freedom from emotional suffering. Suffering sucks. And it's usually self-imposed. If I hadn't analyzed the whole situation and taken an honest, hard look at the choices I had made:

1. I may not have taken full responsibility for everything I experienced.

2. I may have continued to suffer from misguided and distorted thoughts of blame and bitterness.

3. I would have missed an opportunity to gain wisdom and grow.

Plus, I probably would have never wanted to speak to Person X again, and that's just not the way I operate. On a personal level, I really like Person X. Person X works hard, is very smart, and has a good heart. Person X had a life and realities outside of our interactions to deal with that I know absolutely nothing about. Person X did the best they could under the circumstances. I wish Person X nothing but the best and appreciate all their efforts to help us execute our event.

I yanked myself out of my negative and inaccurate mindset about the event. No way did I want to carry around a bag of negative emotional crap from a past situation. What for? Where's the benefit? So I stopped blaming myself and beating myself up for not meeting the goals set (aka wallowing and self-abusing), and I am able to enjoy my present, unburdened with baggage and misconceptions, and armed with fresh wisdom. I kept the best and discarded the rest.

THOUGHT 4: STOP THE BLAME GAME AND SET YOURSELF FREE

You can't feel free if you think that your suffering is caused or controlled by someone else and you haul that sack of crap with you into each new day and each new situation. Our own thinking is what makes us prisoners of our emotions, so changing our thinking is how we set ourselves free. When I analyzed my thoughts and actions about Person X, then broadened my perspective, accepted responsibility for my choices, and moved on without blame for others or myself, I set myself free. You don't have to suffer and haul that suffering into your future. You can change your mind and you can change your life.

THOUGHT 5: DECISIONS, DECISIONS...

If you really think about it, every moment of every day is a continual decision-making process. We don't have to let what we thought and chose yesterday be what we think and choose today. We get used to doing so many of the same things and dragging so many of our same old thoughts and attitudes into each new day that we end up being on autopilot. We actually forget that we can decide on and choose our every move and thought instead of always letting our default action and thinking reign freely.

Start noticing that you are making choices every single day about every little thing you do and don't do, think and don't think. Noticing the big stuff is easy, but if we practice noticing the small stuff, too, it helps us:

WAKE UP – and experience a more consistent sense of freedom because we recognize we are choosing

STAY AWAKE – because by becoming aware of what we're doing and thinking at any given moment we become better equipped to take ownership of the decisions – big and small – that impact our lives. The decisions don't just happen to us.

This awareness of your decision-making is one way to reclaim your sense of freedom, which motivates and inspires you to take charge of your life maze. I think we all have freedoms that we forget we have: to make new choices and new decisions, and to feel differently and think differently. We have the freedom to be happier without physically changing anything, but just by changing our perspective.

It's amazing how much of an impact a mental shift can have on how you feel about your life or a particular situation. To practice this awareness, keep a little notepad with you and jot down the decisions and choices you make throughout your day. Record even the littlest things, like what outfit to wear, whether or not to leave early for an appointment, that you will try to smile all day, or not to get upset about something. (Feel free to download a form to use from my website: www.loreebischoff.com) If you do this for a few days you will be amazed at how freeing and empowering pumping up your "awareness muscle" feels.

One of my clients was a businesswoman with her own retail shop. She used to get so upset when customers would leave the clothes they tried on in a heap on the floor. She viewed this as a personal attack on her, because from her perspective, her store was an extension of herself. She created it. It was her baby. So whenever she felt like it was being disrespected or mistreated, she took it very personally. She imagined that the lack of respect for her property must mean a lack of respect for her. She felt bad and resentful toward these customers.

She finally shifted her perspective by taking her thoughts about what she imagined was occurring out of the picture and just looking at what the picture really was. Without those distorted thoughts creating unpleasant emotions, she was able to understand that how customers treated the merchandise in her store had nothing to do with what they thought about her or her store. Their sloppy behavior was just that – sloppy behavior – not a personal attack. There was nothing more to it. All the rest was in her imagination.

So to end her self-inflicted suffering, she changed her perspective to one that didn't judge, and she learned how to veto thoughts that had no basis in what was actually true. She came to understand that not all of her customers will treat her store like it's their baby, too – because it's not. But it's not personal. It has nothing to do with what they think about her or her store. Now when someone leaves a mess, she just picks it up – without all the judgment and negative emotions that she used to conjure up. It's her beautiful store, which she created, and dealing with sloppy customers comes with the territory. Now she shrugs it off, does what she needs to do to keep her store neat, loves the fact that she has customers, and gets on with her day. Now how freeing is that? One small shift in the way she viewed the situation, and that emotional suffering was gone.

THOUGHT 6: LOVE'S A ONE-WAY TICKET

Loving and appreciating what we have right now also goes a long way toward maintaining a healthy perspective. Noticing and finding pleasure in what you may think are just small, insignificant, and even (sometimes) annoying things helps you realize what's already amazing about your life. After all, our lives are mostly comprised of one small moment after another, with big events occurring only every now and then. It's kind of a waste to wait for the big stuff to be happy about.

Stop right now and think – actually make a list – of ten LITTLE things that you love about your life (or download a form my website: www.loreebischoff.com). (And, no, of course you don't *have* to make a list; I'm just a list-making freak, so that's what I do. But hey, often when I look at my list again before I go to bed, I fall asleep with a smile on my face.) The things you love could be as little as "my third toe," "the fresh wildflowers on my table," or "the view out my window."

Here's the thing: Loving something – anything – just feels good, even if it doesn't love you back. Love is just like giving presents. The best, most fulfilling part is the giving. I could care less if I get a gift back. It's a completely satisfying one-way ticket.

I'll give you some examples of what's on my "top ten" list. I never get tired of these:

- The smell of fresh coffee brewing. I loved waking up to it when I spent time with my grandma as a child and I love waking up to it now (bonus for me that my amazing hubby always brings me a cup in bed).
- The way my favorite pair of blue jeans feel when I put them on
- Seeing beautiful sunsets, dark, raging thunderstorms, and the stars in the sky at night.
- Having the choice to sit and write or read whatever I want to
- Going out for a walk to wherever I want
- The freedom to be as productive as I want to be
- Choosing to tackle my responsibilities with joy
- Choosing to learn more about anything I want, any time, or just chilling and watch a movie that makes me laugh
- My taste buds… oh, how I love those!
- The pretty, yummy-smelling candle on my desk
- Watching out my windows for the local wildlife to make an appearance

And these are just a few of the little things! I have lists of the big things, too, like my husband and children, family and friends, etc. Life is amazing.

THOUGHT 7: I'M SURE YOU CAN THINK OF SOMETHING

If you are still struggling with finding what's already amazing in your life, try this comparison on for some perspective. It's a snapshot of what life is like for the citizens of North Korea:

The government maintains absolute control over any and all information made available to the citizens at all times. This means books, television, radio, newspapers, etc. All forms of media deliver only messages crafted or condoned by the government. You have no choice in what you hear, see, read or believe. Travel outside your village is severely restricted. Your life is 100% controlled by the government. You are allowed zero individualism; it is literally, systematically destroyed. You don't have the luxury of expanding your thinking or making choices for yourself. Because the regime has complete control and influence over you from birth, you can't even imagine a way out. You have no idea how much freedom and abundance exists just a few hours away.

I included this passage not to make you feel guilty, as that would be counter-productive, but to help with your perspective on what's amazing in your life.

Being grateful for what you already have is the foundation. Build on that, and open your eyes and your heart wider to look for amazing things where you may never have thought to look before. What constitutes "amazing" is subjective. It might be making that last mortgage payment and finally owning your home free and clear. It might mean two bowls of rice in one day instead of just one. Just food for thought – how amazing that we get to express our thoughts without fear.

If you don't appreciate the little things, you either won't appreciate the bigger things (for long), or worse yet, when a big amazing thing does come into your life, you either won't recognize it, or that same old mindset and behavior pattern will cause you to neglect it, screw it up, or lose it.

THOUGHT 8: CONNECT THE DOTS

Have you ever been in a situation or gone through an experience and found yourself thinking, "How the heck did that happen? How did I get here? It seemed so good at the beginning and now it's turning into an ugly mess!"

This is what happens to an overwhelming number of lottery winners. Whether they win $3 million or $300 million, they end up broke and right back in the same place they started from (or worse). When this new, life-changing opportunity presents itself, they unwittingly sabotage it because they don't understand that they must expand and modify their thinking and behavior to be able to successfully manage and enjoy the new opportunity. They must grow by learning how to handle their new money and the people in their lives in order to have the best chance at maintaining a long, healthy relationship with their money.

We tend to make the same mistakes with relationships. Let's read some of that paragraph again but swap out the words *opportunity* and *money* with the word *relationship*:

When this new, life-changing relationship presents itself, they unwittingly sabotage it because they don't understand that they must expand and modify their thinking and behavior to be able to successfully manage and enjoy the new relationship. They must grow by learning how to handle their new relationship and the people in their lives in order to have the best chance at maintaining a long, healthy connection.

Old patterns of thinking and behavior will sabotage your new money, your new relationship, your new opportunity, your new whatever if *you* don't modify *your* approach by identifying and changing *your own* old, restrictive patterns.

THOUGHT 9: WHOM TO FOCUS ON

As you're gazing down at your life, make it your mission to identify your behavior patterns. This requires you to spend time reflecting, because if you want to redesign your life maze into something fresh and new, you can't auto-default to your old design scheme. If you truly want to grow and evolve you have to learn about yourself, overcome the endless distractions that keep you from focusing your efforts, and make at least a little time for your own expansion. It doesn't have to be a lot of time; it's more valuable to keep learning consistently and continuously.

Think about how your life has evolved. If you could connect the dots between the significant experiences and phases in your life, what would that line look like? Is it a steadily ascending line with maybe a few dips here and there? Is it a one-step-forward-two-steps-back pattern? Does it look like a bunch of circles and spirals? Perhaps a little of each depending on where you were at a certain time?

By taking the time to picture your life maze from high above, you can learn a lot about yourself. You can see when you were consciously creating your direction and when you were sleepwalking; when you activated a plan and when you just drifted; when you moved in a direction with intense purpose and when you gave the wheel to someone or something else and ended up either in a wonderful new adventure or a place you did not like. Being willing to see the truth of your patterns allows you to see how your life maze was created. As your awareness of your patterns grows, you can embrace what serves you and works for you and change what sabotages you.

Once you've pinpointed what you're doing or not doing that's keeping you from going in the direction you want to go, you can address it (or him or her, as the case may be). Don't shine your spotlight on others' lives, just FOCUS ON YOUR OWN. You have to take ownership of your behavior, choices, and attitude.

Now get some spunk! Determine that you are worth the effort and that *you* want to be the one calling the shots. Commit to pursuing your own betterment and redesigning your life maze from something that is unacceptable or no longer pleases you to something that does – something that is more amazing.

Really think about this: How much more of your life do you want to waste stuck in a negative, unhappy, miserable maze? Or maybe your maze isn't miserable at all. Maybe it's just so-so. Have you compromised your life into a maze of mediocrity? Some people have an amazing life staring them in the face but they don't realize it until they experience the loss of it, or someone in it. Just ask or read about someone who's had a near-death experience, or someone who has lost the love of their life. If you're already aware that your life is amazing, bravo! Carry on!

Once you've decided to pursue something better, don't let your focus shift to past failures or fear of future ones, but instead focus on your strengths and where you want to go. Then be open and willing to learn what you need to help you get there.

Life is one big chain of experiences. By deciding how to feel about your experiences, you will either create your joy or create your suffering. Elevate your perspective, and remember, it's not necessarily the experience itself that's critical, but how you decide to feel about it and what you do with it – no matter how simple or complex it might be.

SUMMARY, PRINCIPLE 3 – MAKE SHIFT HAPPEN

1. Visualize an elevated perspective.
2. Analyze your intentions and what your attention is on.
3. Pump up your awareness muscle.
4. Make your "top ten" list.
5. Become aware of your behavior patterns.
6. Keep your focus where it belongs.

PRINCIPLE 4

change your
CHAIN

"I've never met a person, I don't care what his condition, in whom I could not see possibilities. I don't care how much a man may; consider himself a failure, I believe in him, for he can change the thing that is wrong in his life any time he is ready and prepared to do it. Whenever he develops the desire, he can take away from his life the thing that is defeating it. The capacity for reformation and change lies within."

⁕ PRESTON BRADLEY ⁕

THOUGHT 1: BREAK THOSE CHAINS!

We've talked about changing your perspective – changing your VIEW. Now we're going to talk about changing your chain – changing what you DO.

Is there something you're chained to that's keeping you from what you want to do, be, or have? Is there something holding you back that you drag along with you like a ball and chain? Let's talk about dropping it, unhooking it, breaking it, dissolving it, releasing it – whatever the case may be. Let's shine a spotlight on it and see if you can unchain yourself from it.

What are you chained to that you're itching to change?

THOUGHT 2: CHOICES DON'T HAVE TO BE COMPLICATED

I have a necklace that was annoying me, and it turned out to be a metaphor and inspiration for this chapter.

My husband bought it for me and it's a beautiful, one-of-a-kind piece of art – a pretty pendant on a chain. Each time I wore it, though, the chain worked its way around to the left and the clasp became entangled with the pendant. I was constantly fiddling with it and checking to see if it was still in place. Well, naturally it got to be so frustrating and such a distracting nuisance that I began to wear it less and less often. Pretty soon it just sat in the drawer.

It seemed like such a shame to keep my pretty necklace in the drawer where no one could admire the artist's creation; it was made to be seen. One day I had a simple yet profound thought: Why don't I just change the chain? Duh! I actually felt simultaneously stupid (just for a moment) and excited that I might have found the perfect solution. I remembered a local boutique I had walked by many times where a woman made jewelry. So I took my necklace to her and explained my dilemma. Within a few minutes she had found a perfect replacement for my problem chain, and voilà, problem solved. My lovely pendant gets to fulfill its purpose now – to be seen – and I get to enjoy wearing it knowing that it won't keep going off the track, preventing me and others from enjoying it.

I don't know why I hadn't thought of changing the chain right off the bat, and I began to ponder how often we do the same thing with respect to how we live our lives: let something as simple as a chain keep us from doing something we really want to do, from experiencing something we really want to experience, or even from becoming something we really want to become.

THOUGHT 3: IDENTIFY YOUR CHAIN(S)

Your chain could be something you repeatedly let control your actions in a negative or unproductive way, or something that hinders you from taking a positive action. It can take the form of a commitment you've made and have outgrown, or a precedent you've set that you feel stuck with. It may be habitually destructive behavior, pessimistic thoughts, or even a negatively influential person you've allowed into your life.

I had almost allowed an actual, physical chain to prevent me from doing something I wanted to do – wear my necklace. It seemed like such an easy solution when the light bulb came on and I thought, "Hey, I'm just gonna change that freakin' chain so I can wear my freakin' necklace!" Now of course it's not always that easy to change an emotional or situational chain. But the example of the necklace chain demonstrates how we let things control us when we don't have to. The solution might be an obvious one, like just changing the chain, but affecting the change can certainly be more challenging depending on the situation.

If you find yourself being pulled in a direction in which you really don't want to go, don't just put your desire in a drawer. Ask yourself if you are tethered to something that is hindering your expression of what you want your life to be. Change your chain by identifying what is pulling you off course and then swapping it out for something that supports your direction.

The artist certainly didn't create my necklace to have it hidden away in a drawer never to be worn or seen, and I don't believe you were born to hide your expression of your true self from the world and not flourish. We all want to be seen and we all need to be significant in some way. Don't be shy. Lose your chains.

THOUGHT 4: A BAD HABITUDE

We are all creatures of habit and have our own unique characteristics. Many of these habits and characteristics are good, and at their best they empower us and propel us through life in constructive ways. But at their worst they can hamper our ability to become our best self or even destroy us. We may want to change something about our life – we may dream of a healthier self, a wonderful relationship, or a more fulfilling job. We may even go so far as to seek out self-help and personal growth information. We may know all the steps to take and it sounds great! But too often we don't actually do anything with that information, or we try it for a little while but it doesn't seem to work for us.

There are lots of reasons that we go so far as to seek, gather, and study new strategies for implementing change in our lives, but then don't follow through or have much success. Why? Fear, insecurities, addictions, lack of support, lack of commitment, instructions that are too complicated or incomplete, fear of failure, fear of success, fear of change, fear of shifting focus from one area and directing it to another, low self-worth… did I mention fear?

Some try to implement change but give up when they don't see results fast enough, deciding that the method used won't work for them because it's just not in their character or not the way they work. They confuse habits with aspects of their character. They might say, "I'm just stubborn and stuck in my own ways. I know what works for me and I need to have X, Y, or Z to get from point A to point B." Or maybe it's just not the right time, the right season, the right temperature, the right mood, the right support, the right day of the week, blah, blah, blah. If this sounds familiar, then perhaps you've simply developed a bad habitude! Yes, I said "habitude." It is a word; I looked it up. It means a habitual tendency or way of behaving – about the same thing as *habit*, but it's so much more descriptive with the idea of *attitude* built right into the word. Are your reasons for delaying opportunities for change and growth really excuses in disguise? Are you just stubbornly attached to a bad habitude? It could be part of your character or it could just be years of practicing habituated ways of being.

If being stuck in your ways and knowing what works for you… actually works for you… perfect, keep doing that! Those are routines – also known as habits – and when applied in constructive ways, they can serve you well. But just because a habit or routine worked well for you twenty years ago doesn't mean it still works the same magic now. Things change. We change. Circumstances change. So if you are not happy and that logic is the reason you don't move forward or realize the things you fantasize about, perhaps it's time to face the possibility that you have an entrenched habit that served you well at one time but is now hindering or even harming you. A habit is not a part of your character that you have no control over, and it is often an excuse to give up. By subscribing to the notion that "that's the way I've always done it," you are allowing your past behavior to dictate your future (the one you'd like to have). If you feel you are in a rut that you can't seem to get out of and use the excuse that you are stuck in your ways, you are absolutely right. You are. Stuck. Yuck. By letting your own stubborn mindset keep you from your best life you are letting a badass habit use the hell out of you.

THOUGHT 5: LOOK DEEPER

Try yanking yourself out of your rut by applying your stubbornness – or any other characteristics that have run amok and are now working against you as bad habits – to the development of some *new* habits, ones that actually help you instead of hinder you. Give yourself ample time and maintain consistency when trying to develop new constructive habits. They say it takes about twenty-one consecutive days to form a new habit. If you can practice your new habit for a minimum of fifteen minutes a day for twenty-one days, it's more likely to become a part of your lifestyle. If it's something you've tried unsuccessfully to do before, maybe it's time to turn the spotlight on your self-image. Not succeeding at something doesn't mean you are a failure; you only fail when you stop trying. What you believe about yourself has been developing since childhood through all of your experiences and interactions with others. This, then, becomes your truth.

Maxwell Maltz, in his book *Psycho-Cybernetics*, says, "The self-image then controls what you can and cannot accomplish, what is difficult or easy for you, even how others respond to you just as certainly and scientifically as a thermostat controls the temperature in your home. Specifically, all your actions, feelings, behavior, even your abilities, are always consistent with this self-image."

To have the best chance of success in developing new patterns and habits, we need to examine our self-image and make sure that what we think and believe deep down about ourselves and our capabilities is not in opposition to, but aligned with, the new ways we want to think and act. If you have hindering, negative thoughts about yourself, it's time to examine them, find out why you have them and where they came from, and, most important, determine whether they are really true or if you've just blindly accepted them as true. Again, just because you've held a belief about yourself for a long time doesn't make it true. Just because someone you loved, trusted, or thought was smarter than you told you that you were not attractive, likeable, capable, good enough, smart enough, etc., doesn't make it true; it just makes them ignorant.

THOUGHT 6: SINK OR SWIM

Here's one of my I-can't-do-that stories: Swimming – ugh, I just hated it when I was a kid. I did not like swimming lessons or swimming in lakes – anything that required surviving in water over my head – because I couldn't really swim. I just did not have the ability to hang out and frolic in the deep water. I sank. I was okay in pools because I could hold on to the edge, but for the most part I could not swim and really didn't see the point of putting myself through the misery of trying to learn, as I had no plans of becoming a lifeguard, joining the coast guard, or getting a job as a dolphin wrangler at Sea World. Any profession that required swimming was definitely on my not-to-do list.

One day when I was about sixteen, I was out on a boat in the middle of a lake with a bunch of friends. (*Most* of them were friends anyway.) I had promised to hang on to my friend's sunglasses while she was swimming. I was sitting there in the boat, holding the sunglasses and catching some rays, when all of a sudden this guy (I never did like this guy) walked over, picked me up, and launched me off the boat like he was an Olympic shot-putter. I yelled, "Nooo – I can't swiiimmm…" as I flew through the air. Then I was under water – still holding the sunglasses, by the way, 'cuz that's just how responsible I am!

When I surfaced I saw that this gigantic a-hole of a guy had literally thrown me about twenty feet from the boat! Who does that? So guess what I did? (not too hard to figure out that I didn't drown) – I swam back to the freakin' boat. Who knew?

As I reached the edge of the boat I was simultaneously mystified, relieved, and fuming. "How the heck did I do that?" "Thank God I made it back to the damn boat!" and "I want to kill that s.o.b!" were the thoughts vying for space in my waterlogged brain.

Then the big fat jerk reached down, lifted me out of the water, and set me back into the boat. I yelled at him and he laughed it off. Infuriating! What was I to do? It wasn't like there was going to be any payback, as he was about 6'2" and at least 240 pounds. I measured up to a whopping 5'2" and about 94 pounds – maybe 96 now that I was soaking wet! So I was stuck with my rage and indignation.

But I know that you know what really happened: I realized I could swim. Without thinking, I did something I had previously thought I couldn't do. I believed I could not swim in a lake but I was WRONG. I could. I was capable. And as I sat down and reached for a towel I noticed I was still clutching the sunglasses!

My fear of swimming pretty much dissipated after that little episode. I still don't like swimming, but I can do it. And I definitely know I won't drown if I find myself being flung off a boat by some big fat jerk. (By the way, I say that with gratitude – not affection, but gratitude.)

Challenge the beliefs you have about yourself by asking yourself if they are really true. Is it possible that you might be mistaken? Could you have just blindly believed something and then fulfilled that belief? Is there any good reason to continue clinging to a belief that's making you feel bad, undeserving, or incapable?

The habits and thought patterns you're trying to replace have probably been part of you for many years. This is a process to embark upon with the faith and determination that you can and will create new habits or reshape sabotaging characteristics into ones that that serve you well, however long that may take. It doesn't do you any good to know about positive strategies and processes if you don't apply them in your life. Don't be a victim of your own limiting habits or characteristics.

THOUGHT 7: PRISON MAZE – YUCK!

Sometimes we can become prisoners in our own mazes. We become entangled in so many vine-like chains that we begin to feel weighed down, helpless, and immobilized. Maybe you've over-scheduled your time and made too many commitments, you're financially over-extended, or you're devoting tons of energy to worrying about the past or the future.

You can also become a prisoner in your own maze by building its walls so high and thick that you become isolated. You can't see out and no one new is allowed to see or get in. So you spend much of your time reacting, resenting, and repeating the same negative cycles because you just don't know what else to do or which way to turn! You don't want to let people down. You don't want to rock the boat, afraid you'll end up worse off. Or you want to keep up appearances and not let anyone know that everything is not fine! You just can't seem to find the key that unlocks the door to freedom. You may want to just run away, but don't throw the baby out with the bath water! Don't be so blinded by the things you no longer want in your life that you destroy or abandon the good things in it! What you really need is to find a way to move beyond the situation – to keep the best and discard the rest. The Life A-Mazing Principles can help you do just that.

THOUGHT 8: IF YOU NEED EXTRA HELP

There are some things that are just too complicated or are beyond our ability to change without some outside help. If you have serious dependency problems that you've been trying unsuccessfully to change on your own, I urge you to get a copy of *The Alcoholism and Addiction Cure* by Chris Prentiss. This book provides an enlightened and common-sense look at the reasons people become dependent on drugs, alcohol, or addictive behaviors, and offers a step-by-step holistic approach to becoming free of addiction. "Alcohol and drugs are not the problems; they are what people are using to help themselves cope with the problems," says Chris Prentiss, and "when the underlying problems are discovered and cured, the need for alcohol or drugs disappears." Addictive behaviors include smoking, excessive eating, shopping, gambling, sex, working, and others. If this rings true for you or someone you are close to, please have a look at this book.

THOUGHT 9: ESCAPE THE CHAINS THAT BIND YOU

We need to decide what we want and don't want, and engage. How?

THINK:	Move your thoughts
DECIDE:	Remove the chains hindering decisions
VISUALIZE:	Movie-making time
RELAX:	Stop moving
TAKE ACTION:	Move worry-free

Make a plan and make a move. Little moves, big moves, they all count. Walk or run – either way, just keep putting one foot in front of the other and stay focused on your destination.

When you drive a car or ride a motorcycle or a bike, you learn that your steering follows the direction you're looking in. So if you want to turn left, you need to look to the left. If you don't want to drive off the cliff on your right, don't focus long and hard on the cliff on your right.

THINK

Think about what you really want to keep in your life, what you really don't want to keep in your life, what you want more of, and what you want less of. Write everything down – big things, little things, and things you might not be sure of. "Arghh – yet another list!" you may be thinking. Yes, if you're inspired – even just a little – get a pen right now and start writing! You may be thinking, "Oh sure, like list-making can change my life." And to that I say, "Yes, it absolutely can." If you crave evolving or escaping badly enough, you'll be willing to try whatever it takes to transform your life. Your list should have four sections: one for what you want to keep in your life, one for what you want to discard, one for what you want more of, and one for what you want less of. (Yes, if you'd like one, there is a worksheet for this exercise at www.loreebischoff.com.) This is your brainstorming list, not necessarily your final list; write down everything that comes to mind.

It can actually make you feel a little less weighed down if you get your thoughts out of your head and onto paper or into your computer. This also allows you to herd your thoughts so they're not just running wild on you.

DECIDE

Next, remove the mental or situational chains that are holding you back and proceed as if what you want is possible. Start making decisions about the things you wrote on your lists. Seeing everything in front of you organized in those four categories will help you sort through all the clutter in your mind and get clear on what you want and what you don't want. Weed through your lists and firmly decide what you want to get serious about.

Examples of some things that could end up on your "want to keep" list might be your relationship, job, house, sense of humor, etc. Things that might end up on your "don't want to keep" list could be a car that's nickel-and-diming you, too many commitments, half the stuff in your closet, false beliefs, etc. Your more/less categories might look like: more exercise, reading, time with so-and-so, education, hobbies, and less sugar, fear, cooking, financial burdens, negative attitude... you get the idea.

VISUALIZE

The third step is movie-making. This is the practice of picturing in your mind the results you desire. Many successful athletes and businesspeople tell us that the consistent practice of visualizing how you want to perform and the results you want to achieve is an extremely valuable tool that they've incorporated into their lives. Get a clear vision of what you are striving for and run that scene over and over like a movie in your mind. Do this daily. Don't visualize what you don't want to happen – like that cliff on your right that you don't want to drive off of. You are much more likely to get what you think about and visualize intensely, so obviously it's counterproductive (and depressing) to think intensely about what you don't want to occur.

RELAX

Next, allow your subconscious to get creative and do some of the work for you. The same goes for the Universe, God, or your higher power. Give divine wisdom and guidance a relaxed, open channel through which to connect with and help you. You just constrict the flow when you worry and stress, and it is not a productive or pleasant state to be in. It's quite fantastic how sometimes things finally start to come together when we stop worrying and trying so hard to force them. Keep your eye on the target, but take a deep breath, chill, and give ideas and opportunities a chance to come to you.

ACTION

Finally, once your thoughts are organized in order of importance and you have a clear vision in your mind, it's easier to see what steps you can take toward your goals. There may be some obvious things you can start doing right away, but there may also be some unexpected things that present themselves, so be ready to take steps and make moves when opportunity knocks or inspiration strikes. You need to be willing to be fearless, commit, and follow through.

Let the process flow without getting attached to the outcome! Once you have your vision and your preferences, and you've done all you can do in your stress-free and worry-free state of mind, be okay with whatever outcome happens. It may not be as you pictured it, but it just might be something even better, or something necessary for your growth and evolution that hadn't occurred to you before. Hold your best visions with enthusiasm, engage in and ENJOY the process, and know that's the best you can do and that what will be will be.

I know from personal experience that if your intention is true, you keep your eye on your target, and these things are written down, miraculous things can occur. It's happened to me and others many, many times. I have made lists and vision boards and then tucked them away, only to find them years later and see that everything on them had come to pass. Seriously!

Don't know what you want, or can no longer find what you're passionate about? In their book, *The Passion Test*, Janet and Chris Attwood present a wonderful and easy-to-follow process to help you fine-tune what you want and what your passions are. I actually did the recommended homework in the book and loved it! I found it to be extremely inspiring and helpful, and I can't recommend it highly enough.

THOUGHT 10: OH, THAT HURTS. THINK I'LL HAVE SOME MORE.

Have you ever felt like banging your head against the wall because you somehow wind up in the same type of frustrating situation over and over? Have you said to yourself, "I knew this would happen again," or "Why does this keep happening to me?" but you either can't find an answer, don't spend enough time thinking deeply to answer, or come up with an answer that doesn't address the part of the equation you're responsible for? Sometimes we can actually get addicted to this pleasure/pain behavior. Weird, huh? But oh, so true.

One of my clients was like this. She was spending valuable time and resources searching for more things to get pissed off about in her already dysfunctional relationship. When she found something that upset her she'd have this satisfying aha! moment. For that moment she was gleeful that her efforts paid off, but then the pain set in as she was, of course, hurt and angry at the discovery. Her actions went on for some time until finally at one of our sessions, when I thought she was ready, I pointed out the pattern she had developed and suggested that she seemed to be rather addicted to the pleasure of seeking out and finding pain. I asked, "Why then don't you stop doing that and do something that doesn't hurt? Maybe even something that feels good – like working on yourself?" I suggested she stop spending so much of her time looking for things to get angry about and instead use that time to start learning how to be the person she said she wanted to be and creating the life she wanted to have. A light flashed across her consciousness so brightly that I could see it beaming right through her eyes, and she had the guts to admit to her pleasure/pain addiction.

What had her focus on blaming others for her unhappiness gotten her? Exactly what she was looking for: misery and pain. There are times in our lives when things happen that make us feel miserable. That's just an undeniable part of life. Sometimes we need to be miserable for a bit because that's how we process things. Then we get tired of being miserable and seek to feel good. Knowing what *miserable* feels like helps us really appreciate feeling good.

But if we're not careful we can develop a lifelong pattern of being miserable. You might think, "Who in their right mind wants to be miserable all the time?" You'd be surprised. If you're miserable most of the time and you don't do everything you can to change that state of being, then perhaps there's a benefit hidden in there somewhere. It's just possible that being miserable or depressed all the time is fulfilling certain needs. People can actually experience a sense of comfort from it. It's familiar, and we like familiar. It's a way of exercising control over ourselves that no one else can. Other people feel bad for us and want to comfort us. We become a source of concern to them so we feel significant. We can even manipulate others by making them feel like they have to tread carefully lest they upset us.

Many people who are unhappy or depressed attach themselves to the story that it's someone else's fault and therefore out of their control, which alleviates them from the responsibility of creating change. But even if you were a victim of someone's bad choice at one time, that doesn't relieve you of the responsibility of turning your life around and correcting its course. The ball is now in your court. If you spend all day cooking up a pot of misery stew, guess what you're going to be eating for dinner. Guess what you're serving up to those around you. But you can decide to serve up something better at any given moment.

Examine carefully what you are getting out of feeling this way. Search deeply to find the hidden benefit that makes it a difficult state to dislodge yourself from. You may surprise yourself. And once you discover that you might be responding to a need, you can search for a positive way to address that need and begin to transition out of the negative state.

THOUGHT 11: NO CARRY-ON BAGGAGE

Baggage is just one more ingredient we throw into that pot of misery stew (such as refusing to forgive, holding a grudge, punishing ourselves for past behavior, punishing others for past behavior, etc.). Honest to God, the baggage we choose to carry around is staggering. It's like a big fat pair of cement shoes that just keeps us weighed down in a murky, suffocating place, making forward steps nearly impossible. You just can't move forward if you refuse to let go of the bag on your back that has been filling up with crap, sometimes for decades! You are keeping negative things from the past alive and well if you don't just drop it. Hold onto it long enough and tightly enough, and like those cement shoes, it'll take you nowhere but down, Baby. And that ride sucks. Put your baggage on your "don't want to keep" list.

THOUGHT 12: OH, JUST GIVE IT UP ALREADY

Here's an interesting and amusing observation I made. (Animal enthusiasts will appreciate this.) We had two pet cats, Taz and Casper. They were best buds – most of the time. If you've ever had a cat, you know that they sleep a lot – at least sixteen hours a day. One of the most coveted catnapping spots in our house is on the tile floor directly in front of the refrigerator, because it's toasty warm there.

Frequently Taz would be snoozing away there when Casper decided he wanted the spot. So naturally what he did was pick a fight. It was cleverly disguised as an affectionate "let me groom you" gesture. He'd walk up to a peacefully sleeping Taz and start to lick his head and nuzzle him, which, of course, evolved into a friendly wrestling match and eventually resulted in an all-out battle for the toasty fridge spot. Taz would play along and wrestle for a while, but he ultimately gave in every time. He'd look at Casper as if to say, "Fine, I don't give a rat's ass. You take the stupid spot." Then he would simply go find a softer, more comfy spot on the bed and resume his nap. He wasn't willing to invest all his resources (time, energy, and emotions – if cats have those) in trying to hang on to something that wasn't really worth hanging on to. He knew when to say "when" and simply move on to something that was just as good or better.

The moral of the story is that sometimes the choice to surrender ultimately affords you a better result than trying to hang on to something which is resisting you, causing you grief, or draining all your resources. Don't allow yourself to be a doormat or deem yourself a failure, but just let go of the problem and move on to something better, or be open so that something better can come into your life. Think strategy and freedom, not ego and fear, and redirect where and how you spend your resources. Change your chain!

SUMMARY, PRINCIPLE 4 – CHANGE YOUR CHAIN

1. Identify your chains.
2. Investigate your beliefs.
3. Determine priorities for what you want and don't want.
4. Establish and commit to action steps.
5. Remove cement shoes.
6. Surrender.

PRINCIPLE 5

ROMANCE
your life

"To love one's self is the beginning of a life-long romance."
❉ OSCAR WILDE ❉

THOUGHT 1: FALL IN LOVE WITH YOURSELF

Start falling in love with yourself, one step at a time, by romancing your life. This means treat your life, your time, and your SELF with as much respect and importance as someone you dearly love, greatly revere, and/or are really trying to impress!

I like to think of this as romancing your life. Think about when you first start seeing someone you're really excited about. When you romance another person, you put your best foot forward. You present your best self so they can experience the best of you. You pay extra attention to your grooming. You are respectful, considerate, and conscientious. You give the other person your time, attention, and energy, and act with integrity. You have the intention of making the time you spend together fun and fulfilling. It's all so very romantic! Not only the "dates," but even the intentions you have and the processes you go through to prepare for the dates are romantic. These processes and intentions are something we embark upon with the goal of pleasing the other person by *being* pleasing. It's an intoxicating and wonderful state of bliss to be in. It simply feels good.

That's a feeling I want to experience as much as possible! I don't want to have to wait around for opportunities to have that feeling only through encounters with others. Those processes and intentions can be practiced with the goal of being pleasing to *ourselves*. We can enjoy a romantic state of mind by striving to impress *ourselves*. When I look at myself in the mirror each morning while I'm getting ready for my day, or when I brush my teeth before I go to bed each night, I want to feel good about myself, my attitude, and how I treat myself. Specifically designating some "quality focus" on myself, no matter what my day entails, makes me feel good.

THOUGHT 2: NOURISHMENT FROM THE OUTSIDE IN

What does that quality focus look like? It will not be the same for everyone. For me, it's typically something like this:

PERSONAL GROOMING

Even if I'm not leaving my house and no one is coming over, I still want to care for my appearance, so my grooming routine is practiced religiously. I have a hard time feeling like I'm on top of the world if I live like I'm by myself in a cave and just let things go unattended. I want to look and feel as well-groomed and refreshed as if I were going out with someone or having someone over. I want to be pleasing to myself because what I think and feel about myself is more important than what anyone else thinks.

Since my office is in my home, I have the luxury of not even having to get out of my p.j.'s before I start working. And this does happen frequently. Emails and phone calls start, and before I know it noon is knocking on the door! Even if I'm not going anywhere, I always feel so much better when I get dressed. I am one of those people who dresses according to the mood I'm in, and what I chose to put on influences my mood just as my mood influences my choice of clothing. The point is I don't wear stuff I don't like. It has nothing to do with being dressed up or wearing expensive things; most days I'm in my favorite jeans and t-shirt or gym clothes (they're comfy and I know I'm more likely to work out if I'm already dressed for it!). I get rid of clothing I don't like anymore so it's not cluttering up my space, and I wear things I like to please myself and serve my purposes.

EXERCISE

It never seems as if there's enough time to do all the things I want to do, but I try to fit some type of exercise in as consistently as possible. Sometimes my routine is more frequent and intense than others, but no matter what, I find something physical to do. We all know the benefits of exercise so I don't need to tell you why it's a good idea to do it. I can add this little nugget to help inspire you, though: Our motivation for staying as physically fit and healthy as we can should extend beyond our own, personal benefits. The more we abuse our health and our bodies, allowing ourselves to deteriorate unnecessarily, the more we risk becoming a burden to our families – namely our children. I do not want to require a high level of care from my loved ones because of my own lack of proper care for my physical well-being. It's a different story when care is required due to something beyond our control, but the stuff that is under our control? Well, please think about how the way you're living your life could affect those close to you if you are too careless or neglectful for very long.

HOME

Your home is your sanctuary. I put an enormous amount of thought and focus into my home environment and its maintenance. I know what I need to thrive and what makes me tick, and for me that means my home must be a certain way. I know I function best in a neat, everything-in-its-place environment, so that's what I create in our home. It's not about the size or the price of the furnishings, it's about our home being clean and organized and visually appealing to me and my husband and functional for my family.

Our homes should be our own special places where we can go to rest, recharge our batteries, and feel completely comfortable being ourselves. As I approach my door, I don't want to feel dread about what awaits me on the other side. I want to feel a sigh of relief and like I'm being welcomed with a big hug.

READING

Part of my daily ritual since childhood has been reading. I find reading to be expansive. Every word I read is like food for my brain and my soul, and I grow in some way. It's a practice that allows me to educate myself about anything I want, expand my knowledge base, and expose myself to new topics and ideas. It keeps my communication skills polished and it entertains me. At night it relaxes me, and I go to sleep feeling like I'm a little wiser than I was when I woke up that morning.

These are just a few of the things I do to elevate my spirit. You may have a completely different set of rituals that trip your trigger. Later I'll introduce more ideas about how you can nourish your spirit from the outside in. Whatever standards you set and efforts you make, they should be no less for yourself than what you do to show up for others. What *you* think of you is more important than what others think of you.

Quality focus is a gift we can give ourselves every day. Do you give any of these gifts to *your* life on a regular basis? How much of your attention is actually on your own life?

THOUGHT 3: SO-AND-SO SHOULD...

We all want to experience the best of other people. If you don't enjoy your own company or are not generally pretty happy with your life, then you are not experiencing the best of YOU. And if you aren't experiencing the best of YOU, neither are the rest of us.

I believe we are here to learn, grow, evolve, and strive to become our best selves. We all want to experience the best of *other* people. No one wants to continually be in the company of misery unless misery really does love company, and we already talked about that. One way to eliminate misery from our lives, and hence the world, is by not contributing to it on any level. We can all do our part to have an amazing life in an amazing world, and the common sense place to start is at home, with ourselves.

It's easy for us to become so connected to what's going on in the lives of our friends, family members, and even people in the media who we don't even know, that we stop paying much attention to our own lives. Some of us direct massive amounts of thought and energy to dispensing judgment and advice, thinking up solutions for other peoples' problems, and declaring what we would do if we were in their shoes, blah, blah, blah. Why do we incessantly focus so much on the lives of others? Perhaps it is amusement, or maybe we do this out of fear that we are somehow less important than others and it is a way to elevate ourselves. Maybe it's a desire to feel that we're all in the same boat. Or maybe it's a convenient distraction to keep us from actually having to focus on our own lives and come up with solutions to improve our own lots. We can be a hypocritical bunch, we humans, if we're not careful.

We can do ourselves and others a big favor, and make a positive impact, simply by endeavoring to cease the negative, resource-wasting habit of judging others and deciding what they should do. We have no idea what their path and purpose are all about or how their life maze has been created, just as they have no idea about ours. Each of us contributes to the whole in our own way, so let's focus on contributing our best, because, rest assured, the positive impact will be felt.

THOUGHT 4: SERVE YOURSELF

Romancing your own life means giving your best for yourself, even when there is no one else involved or there to see it. When you give to yourself and focus on becoming your best, you have the best of yourself to share with others. You have the best of yourself with which to provide a role model for your children. And you have the best of yourself to contribute to society. You can't help but feel good practicing the intention of romancing your life!

This is not an expensive endeavor. It doesn't require loads of cash or resources. Just love your life enough to treat it with respect and acknowledge it as an amazing process that you get to create as you go along, moment by moment.

You can romance your own life the same way you romance another person. If you want your life to be filled with love and experiences that fill you with joy, then treat your life like you are DATING IT:

- Pay attention to what you say and how you say it. Be at your best with your thoughts, words, and deeds.
- Commit time, energy, and love to your own evolution and health. Give yourself opportunities to grow, learn, and expand your thinking.

⁕ Make your life fun and beautiful. Make it feel, smell, and taste good. Let your potential fill your senses, like a new romance.

You don't have to invest anything other than your attention and an effort to shift your thinking. Cultivate the best in yourself and be willing to *see* the best in yourself, just like you would hope a first date sees the best in you.

We must all be concerned with our own well-being – physically, spiritually and emotionally – if we truly want to become greater expressions of ourselves and have more fulfilling lives.

THOUGHT 5: VALUES – PAWNED OR PRESERVED?

With a new romance, we have a fresh start with someone. With your life, you get to have a fresh start literally every moment if you want to. In any given second you can change the way you view something, someone, or yourself, and create a fresh start. If you really think about this, it is incredibly empowering.

We frequently ask each other, "How's life treating you?" I think we should consider the question, "How are you treating your life?" How we treat our own lives is a reflection of our deepest values. Sometimes we get so busy living from day to day that we don't pause long enough to thoughtfully consider what our deepest values are. You and/or your values may have changed over time. Maybe, as is common, you just adopted the values of your parents or others in your environment without really thinking much about them. Perhaps you've outgrown old values or adopted new ones, but your approach to life has not reflected those changes, causing you to feel conflicted. Maybe you've drifted away from the basic, core values you learned as a child and don't feel very proud about not honoring them in your life now.

Sometimes we unwittingly devalue ourselves by placing greater value on other people and their objectives than we do on ourselves and our own lives.

It may be time to take stock, examine your values, and determine whether the way you are conducting your life is in sync with them. (If you need a jump-start and want some examples of what some of our most common core values are, go to my website: www.loreebischoff.com.) Jon M. Huntsman has a wonderful book, *Winners Never Cheat*, that is an excellent refresher course in the basic core values that most of us were taught as children and the importance of maintaining those values throughout all you do in life.

THOUGHT 6: TREAT YOURSELF AS LEAST AS WELL AS YOU DO THE DOG OR THE CAR

I'd like you to answer these seven questions (you got it – worksheets at www.loreebischoff.com):

1. Are you nourishing your body with the pride of ownership, treating it with respect and giving it food and activities that serve you well and help you to thrive?

How many people do you know who treat their car or their pets better than they treat themselves? They groom their pets, feed Fluffy the right food, and visit the vet for regular checkups. They wash and wax the car, put the right fuel in the tank, and get the oil changed regularly. They even take Fluffy and the car out for nice walks and drives. The relationships some people have with their pets and cars is very loving and attentive. Why would you treat yourself as less valuable than your car or your pet by neglecting to give your body the attention it deserves? With your body as your vehicle, you can go places, change things, live, love, create…. So it makes good sense to be attentive to yourself by regularly focusing a lot of TLC on yourself – outside and inside.

Your life and *your* journey are just as valuable as *you* decide them to be – certainly more valuable than the car!

2. Are you just methodically going through the motions of getting through each day?

Try to banish the mindset of just getting through the day. That is just not a very fulfilling or fun state of mind. Sometimes you'll hit a speed bump or you'll have to deal with something that makes you want to just survive the day. But that shouldn't be the norm. Think about what you might do if you were out on a bad date. Out of respect you'd finish the date with kindness and integrity, call it a night, and move on – hopefully give it another shot with someone new or with a new approach. You can do that with your life, too. Decide you're going to close this chapter, open a new one, and try a new approach.

To help break the monotony of methodically going through the motions, start your day off by deciding what your purpose for the day is. It could be anything, big or small – like smile more, call your dad, clean out the garage, laugh, maintain an optimistic attitude no matter what, look for a new job, read a classic, start a business, cook a good dinner, jump out of a plane (with a parachute, of course).

3. Do you feel a sense of purpose and that you are fulfilling it?

Feeling a sense of purpose, no matter what it is, motivates us and makes it exciting to get up each day and take part in our lives. Whether it seems big or small, important or insignificant, as long as it serves *you* it has value. I don't care if you're raising chickens or raising children, baking cupcakes or branding cattle. How can you tell if it serves you? By how it makes you feel. If it is fulfilling and isn't harming someone else, then it's serving you well. Nourishing yourself by engaging in that which you find fulfilling is another wonderful way to romance your life.

4. Are you nourishing your spirit? Do you have a connection with your spirit, God, a religion, a larger-than-life resource of some sort?

Obviously spiritual health and focus is very personal, and unique to each of us. There are as many ways to be in touch with one's spirituality as there are people. Exploring different religions and ways of observing, living, or practicing your own form of spirituality is well worth the journey. It helps you keep things in perspective, keep your priorities straight, and maintain a balanced life. A connection with God or something larger than yourself – that limitless, unconditional love and spiritual fuel – can completely fill you up and be downright magical. No matter what happens in life, your spirituality is the one constant that is impervious to change.

5. Are you feeding your mind anything new, anything that *expands your thinking* and helps you grow?

Growth is an essential human need that we all should attend to. If you don't grow, you die – maybe not literally, but spiritually and emotionally. We've all heard stories about people who retired and died soon afterward. They stopped growing, were unable to replace their purpose in life, and could no longer find reasons to get up each day. Even if someone doesn't physically die, they can mentally die by ceasing to engage in life; they simply exist.

When we expose ourselves to new concepts, experiences, and people, we can't help but gain something. We may learn and embrace new ideas or experience something that either challenges our current beliefs or causes us to be even more sure of them. Whatever the case, to truly be fulfilled we absolutely must continue to grow.

6. What kind of physical activity are you incorporating into your lifestyle?

I recently overheard a man telling someone about the weight loss he had achieved over the past year or so. He was so excited about sharing how he did it and the fantastic results he was experiencing, that I asked him to tell me more about it. I thought it might be something I could share with some of my clients who are working on their fitness and health.

He was about sixty and was in great shape. He got up well before the sun each morning and went to the gym. The supplements he was taking were extremely satisfying, promoted his weight loss and energy level, and immensely improved his health. He was even off of his medications as he had managed to reverse the conditions that caused him to need them in the first place! His doctor told him that whatever he was doing, to keep doing it! He had literally grown younger with his new lifestyle of taking such good care of his body. This in turn caused him to feel great emotionally and had a really positive effect on his entire outlook on life! He was a new man and you could just feel his joy and energy resonating from him!

Another person was listening to us and became quite interested as well.

He was extremely overweight (300+ lbs.) and you could tell that for him just breathing was a very labor-intensive act. He was also diabetic and had other health issues on top of that. The interesting thing I observed was that he kept coming up with reasons he couldn't do the things the "new man" had done. Rather than thinking about what he *could* do, he focused only on what he thought he *couldn't* do. He already ate well, so he claimed. He was diabetic so he probably wouldn't be able to take the supplements. His office was in his home, and because he had a particular routine, he wasn't too sure where he'd find the time... blah, blah, blah.

This is a man who said his wife couldn't get him to walk down to the end of the driveway to the mailbox, and the most exercise he got was walking from his in-home office to his living room couch. Yet here he was, attending a work-related event at a sprawling resort that he had to fly to. Hmm – do you think he placed as much value on his health as he did his job?

Where the "new man" and I saw opportunity, he just saw obstacles. He had the chance to try something new, and a willing mentor to guide him, and he wasn't excited! I couldn't help but feel a little sad for him. At the rate he's going he won't be around many more years to make that journey from his office to his couch. I really hope he thought about it more on the flight home and decided to give it a shot. What does he have to lose?

Here's the thing about exercise: You'll have a better chance at getting fit and staying healthy if you don't approach it with the attitude of "I hate the body I've been saddled with and I wish I could change it," but instead with the attitude of "I'm partners with this body I've been born into. It gets me where I want to go and houses my mind and spirit. So I want to care for it and treat it with respect."

Our bodies aren't meant to sit motionless all of the time. They require movement of some sort. If you leave a car sitting immobile, entropy will eventually set in. Same goes with our bodies. Find something physically active you enjoy and give it a shot.

7. Are you in a place you love?

This could mean physically or mentally. Either way, the "place" should be one that you're *willing* to be. Knowing that you're there because you choose to be can give you a certain level of peace because you have chosen it. Even if it's not a place you want to stay, as long as you know you can move through it and grow from what the experience has to offer, it will add value to your life. You can choose to stay and you can choose to move on. Loving or at least being at peace with what you already have puts you in a better state of mind for making changes.

THOUGHT 7: MORE

Open your imagination to the idea that there's more. Trust me – there's AL-WAYS more. We live on a giant ball that somehow just hangs in space. Seriously… a giant, life-sustaining ball suspended in space, which rotates around another giant ball, also suspended in space, which is infinite. For heaven's sake, just look up – there's more than we can possibly see or imagine. Sometimes we need to change the way we *don't* live! What's out there that you aren't you doing that you know you want to do? What might you be looking at that you aren't really seeing?

We can become so accustomed to something that we cease to see the magic in it. Here we all are, millions of us living on this big ball as it spins in space, and we don't even notice this; we certainly don't feel it, and we don't fall (or float?) off of it. The most powerful forces seem to be the ones we can't see, but we still experience them: gravity, wind, love, faith.

The proof that life is amazing is demonstrated by the simple fact that we exist! There is a magical force that starts and keeps our hearts beating, and endows us with the will to survive and to create, and the desire to give love and be loved. That magical force is the romance of life. What is not completely amazing about that?

It shouldn't be hard to believe that there is more to life than you initially thought; that more love, peace of mind, joy, harmony, and abundance is possible for you. First look for the magic and in what you already have and who you already are, and then dare to believe that you can have more and give more.

By the way, having more doesn't mean getting it for nothing. If you want to have more you have to give more. If you want more vibrant health, you must give your health more attention through learning how to improve it and following through with action. If you want more money, you have to activate a plan that includes deciding what service you intend to provide in return for it. If you want more harmony in your relationships, you must give more effort and attention to your role and behavior. If you want to feel pure joy, you have to be more charitable with the resources you have – your time, money, love, attention, knowledge – without expecting something in return. If you want more happiness in your life, you must learn what core things make you happy and BE those things. We live in the infinite, so there is an infinite supply of what we need to be happy.

THOUGHT 8: YOUR ADVENTURE

Try to think of your life as an amazing, grand adventure. In a true adventure there are unknowns. There may be risks and events that tax us and stretch us to our limits. There is the excitement of new discoveries, the joy of accomplishments, and the agony of getting lost and even hurt sometimes. Each step of the way, turn of events, or situation may not seem so grand by itself, but each has its meaning and value and contributes to the quality of your journey and your experience of it.

Don't underestimate the value of any of your experiences, good or bad – especially the bad or uncomfortable ones. Those are the ones that allow you to grow the most. If you keep going down the same painful paths that take you through the same painful experiences, you haven't been analyzing them objectively enough to get the message – what part you have played in the repetitive pattern and what you're supposed to be learning about yourself. Admitting that you had a part in creating these circumstances is the first step in changing them. In order to do that you have to examine your own behavior, past and present – not *other* peoples' behavior. Learning from the experiences of your past means you can apply more wisdom to your present. As you begin owning your past decisions, also be willing to accept what you have already created without judgment and recognize how amazing it is that you now have the awareness to re-create your life maze.

Once you come to terms with your role, accept the gift of the learning, then let it go. You do yourself a great disservice if you beat yourself up about it and carry around hate, blame, and resentment. This just adds more dead weight to the baggage that we discussed earlier. Such thoughts are burdensome, depressing, and destructive. They foster negative emotions and, whether you're aware of it or not, others pick up on that. You can end up repelling positive people and, like a magnet, attracting negative people and experiences to you.

If you truly seek to be happy, free, uplifted, and constructive, make peace with your past so it stops tripping up your future, and flush the hate, blame, and resentment down the toilet with the rest of the tidy bowl contents that don't make your life (or the lives of those you are close to) any better or brighter. Then brush yourself off, smile, and move on. Just be sure to take the gift of what you learned with you.

There may still be times when you suffer and have to tend to things that you'd rather not. We should not walk away from our responsibilities because we imagine that they are keeping us from having an amazing life. What's amazing is that you get to CHOOSE whether or not you will fulfill your obligations and you *can* CHOOSE to do it in a peaceful manner, with pride and integrity. It is possible to subtly re-create your life maze without eliminating everything about your current one.

THOUGHT 9: THE SPEED OF TIME

Sometimes it's the littlest things that bring the biggest smiles. Sift back through some of your memories, and I bet you can recall some that didn't seem grand at the time, but now stand out as fond and wonderful memories.

You had a lot less to do when you were a kid. Your thoughts and focus were probably rooted in whatever you were engaged in at the moment. I don't remember spending a lot of time thinking about the past or the future when I was a child. As children we are much more plugged in to the present moment, so time seems to move more slowly than it does when we get older, but perhaps it's really that we move more slowly through time. If you are speeding through life and can't understand why time goes by so much faster now than it did when you were a kid, it's probably *you* who is doing the speeding. Time hasn't sped up. In fact it hasn't moved at all. It's just there. It isn't really a thing, is it? It's just a brilliant construct we made up so we can function in an organized manner – something that allows us to harmonize and synchronize and not go around crashing into each other!

As adults we have a lot more to do, and an exorbitant amount of our focus is on the past and the future. We move faster and try to fit more in, and half the time we aren't paying attention to what's happening right now! All of a sudden it's New Years again and we wonder, "Where did the year go?" The speed of the passage of time that we experience is actually the speed at which we *choose* to move through it. It's hard to even see any roses, let alone stop and smell them, when you are cruising by them at warp speed, sleepwalking, looking behind you, or having tunnel vision.

One way to prioritize your time is to think about what you would change if you found out you had just six more months to live – aw hell, let's make it six days. Would you make any changes? Would you speed up or slow down? Would you eliminate some things from your to-do list that suddenly don't seem all that important and see your priorities in a new light? Do you think you might place more value on yourself, the quality of your life, and spending your time meaningfully? Would the value of a day – or an hour – change?

To notice how you treat your time, at the end of each day reflect back over it and notice how you feel about it. (If you want to write down your thoughts about these questions, go to www.loreebischoff.com for a worksheet.)

* What was good about your day?
* Were you productive?
* Did you experience any joy?
* Do you remember smiling or laughing?
* Did you spend your time in ways that served you or others?

⁜ Were the things you did of your choosing, or did the day seem like it just happened to you?

⁜ Did you pay attention to the people who are important to you – including yourself?

Don't sweat the small stuff, but don't neglect to *see* the small treasures either. They contribute in a big way to feeling the magic of life.

As I was writing this I took a break to stretch. I walked into the other room and as I passed by my window, I saw a phenomenal sunset. It was turquoise, red, fuchsia, and copper. I took the time to soak it in for just a few minutes. I grabbed a glass of wine, and went outside to sit and watch this amazing gift – just me and the sunset. It was downright romantic and magical – an awe-inspiring and beautiful few moments.

Even if I had had a day that wasn't all I wanted it to be, at least I made time to consciously absorb a magical moment that reminded me to focus on right now, notice something beautiful right in front of me, and smile. Take a little time to romance your life. You're worth it. I swear it's true!

THOUGHT 10: TOOLS

Get into the practice of thinking about your SELF and your life maze every day. It really is like an exercise in that the more you practice, the better you get at it. The better you get at it, the more positive results you will experience. The more positive results you experience, the more you will want to continue doing it.

Two of the positive results you develop from thinking about your self and your life maze every day are AWARENESS and INTENTION.

Let's look at why these two things are important by comparing them to their opposites. AWARENESS means having cognizance – being conscious, awake, and watchful. So the opposite – being unaware – means not being cognizant, not being conscious of one's environment and thoughts, and being without control.

INTENTION is having a course of action that one plans to follow – a purpose or goal that guides action. So not having intention means lacking a specific goal or purpose – having an unplanned day or life.

Hmm – being conscious and having a purpose, or not being in control and lacking goals. Which do you think is more likely to get you where you want to go?

You can see why it's important to exercise awareness and intention on a daily basis if you want to be the creator of your life maze. These tools are free! They are the same tools you would use to plan a romantic evening with someone. They are reminders to be attentive and in control of yourself, to remain aware of your choices and make decisions with purposeful and positive intentions. We all want our lives to be beautiful experiences filled with love, joy, and happiness, and we can endeavor to make that happen by paying attention to what we are thinking and doing.

THOUGHT 11: RED MEANS STOP

You're in your car approaching a busy intersection. The light is red. Do you stop your car? Most likely yes. Why? Because even though at that moment you don't consciously think about all of the consequences of not stopping the car, you do know that if you go through that red light into the traffic moving through the intersection, you will suffer. So to avoid the unnecessary suffering, you follow the rules and stop your car at the red light. Recognizing things you do in your life that you know are going to cause you suffering, and then willing or disciplining yourself to stop, is no different. We can create and follow our own rules just as we follow the rules set up by society. Red light means stop. We stop so we don't hurt ourselves or someone else. What can you stop doing or thinking that is creating suffering in your life or causing suffering for others?

Oh and we know when we're about to blow right into the red light zone. We know that feeling we get when we decide to pick a fight, challenge someone's opinion until we create an argument, lie, cheat, or steal. We know it's wrong and will likely cause some form of suffering for ourselves or someone else. It isn't any different than driving through that red light. We can choose to stop and we can choose to zip it, thereby avoiding all kinds of unnecessary pain and b.s.!

And yes, that does mean sometimes zipping it even when you know you're right about something. You can be right or you can be happy.

How is that romancing your life? I look at it like this: I want to live and be happy and I want to do no harm because I want others to live and be happy, too. See a red light, hear a red siren, feel a red (negative) feeling? Stop. Red means stop. Simple.

THOUGHT 12: WAKE UP, SHOW UP, ENGAGE

Wake up, show up, and engage – I love this concept because it's just so to the point.

WAKE UP TO YOUR LIFE

It's you; it's yours – your journey/process/grand adventure/life maze. We already need to sleep away about a third of it; why would you want to go through the other two-thirds sleepwalking? Snap out of it! Live it like you own your life. You don't need anyone's permission but your own.

SHOW UP FOR YOUR LIFE

Show up each day by being wherever you are with mindfulness. Have you ever been driving and become so completely lost in thought that suddenly you realize you have absolutely no recollection of how you got from point A to point B? You don't remember what you drove past or what traffic signals you unconsciously heeded. Where were you? Certainly not present. Be where you are. Be here now. Don't squander your present moments.

ENGAGE IN YOUR LIFE

To be engaged means to be committed. Be committed to your thoughts and actions. Pay attention! Carry out your actions with conscious thought and good intentions. Your thoughts and actions compose your experiences and create the physical expression of your life. It's important that you know what you're doing. Cultivate your awareness and practice ownership of your life maze. There is infinite joy in the awareness of being awake and actively engaged in doing what you want and/or need to do.

I invite you to find what is amazing about the life maze you have already created and encourage you to delight in the freedom you have to re-create, remodel, or reassemble it in whatever way you want to.

There is a ripple effect from the energy you generate. It goes out into the universe and becomes part of the collective energy. Vow to put out the good energy – the energy of romance, of love, of joy, and of harmony. Peace.

SUMMARY, PRINCIPLE 5 – ROMANCE YOUR LIFE

1. Fall in love with yourself.
2. Revisit your values.
3. Treat yourself right.
4. Access and use your tools.
5. Red means stop.
6. Wake up, show up, engage.

AFTERWORD

Wow – you're finished! Thank you for reading my thoughts. I hope you feel inspired and confident that with the help of the Life A-Mazing Principles you can be a happier person and create a happier life.

The Life A-Mazing Principles can be converted to simple and effective affirmation statements that you can use daily to help keep your thoughts positive and productive. There are examples at the website: www.loreebischoff.com

Now go forth with the knowledge that you possess the ultimate gift: the FREEDOM TO CHOOSE HOW YOU CREATE AND RE-CREATE THE MAZE OF YOUR LIFE.

Warmest,

Loree

ACKNOWLEDGEMENTS

All the people we encounter, from the minute we come into the world until we leave it, contribute in some way to the person we are. Some have had major negative influences on us, some have been a constant source of support and encouragement, and some were there for just a moment but had a critical, lasting impact.

I would like to acknowledge and extend my heartfelt gratitude to the following people who have supported me and influenced my life in ways that contributed to the person I've become and to my writing this book.

To my husband, Eric: Thanks, Honey, for all you do and have done which made it easy for me to do what I love. Your BIG vision, BIG thinking, and I-can-do-that mindset have had a massive influence on me. Thank you for being my partner, my "magic man," and the love of my life.

Thanks to my beautiful mom who was always on my side, allowed me the freedom to become myself, and had the wisdom to expose me to great books throughout my life. That has truly been one of the greatest gifts I've ever received. Your instinct was perfect, Mom, and I love you for having the courage to follow it.

My children, Garett and Montanna, have taught me far more than I have taught them. Being their mother has been the most divine reason that I am the woman I've become. There are no words that can fully describe the love I have for these two amazing people and the immense honor I feel for getting to be their mom. Thank you, my beautiful babies.

I must thank God for blessing me with the best grandmother in the world.

With a strong and steady-as-she-goes countenance, she's been a wonderful demonstration of unconditional love and amazing stamina. The Gram taught me much – not by design – but simply by the way she lived her life. We shared countless hours of fishing on the dock when I was a little girl. She didn't just feed me the fish she caught, but taught me how to fish.

Lynne Klippel and Christine Kloser – these two wonderful, talented women created the "Get Your Book Done" course, and honestly I don't think I'd be writing this acknowledgment right now if I hadn't participated. It was the perfect thing for me to do at the perfect time. Thank you, Ladies.

Gwen Hoffnagle – thank you for kindly but firmly molding my words into a smooth read that still reflects my message. You classed up my creation by cleaning up my sailor mouth yet left just enough of my spice so it remains authentic to my voice and delivery. Muchas gracias.

A gracious thank you to KC Miller, the founder and director of the Southwest Institute of Healing Arts, a spectacularly special place that was a pivotal part of my evolution to the next great phase of my life.

I'd also like to thank Richard Seaman, whose coaching and teaching skills were a vital part of helping me become the coach I am today. Richard, your words of encouragement at just the right time during the writing of this book are so very appreciated.

Elmas Vincent, thank you for your simple but highly impactful statement: "Just write a page a day," which allowed me to know without a doubt that I could indeed write this book. My desire was already there and so were my ideas and my outline. But that single statement flipped a switch in me that shifted what seemed like an overwhelming task into a very manageable process.

A huge thank you to Anthony Robbins, Cloe Madanes and Mark Peysha for creating a fantastic training course that has added immensely to my knowledge base and skill sets. I feel so privileged to have had the opportunity to learn from you.

Kathy Singer, you are a gifted photographer and have captured the perfect photos to represent the message on these pages. Thanks for a great and really fun photo shoot!

about the
AUTHOR

Loree Bischoff received her life coach certification from the Southwest Institute of Healing Arts (SWIHA), Arizona's award-winning private holistic healthcare college. She has been married to the same amazing man since 1984 and they have two wonderful all-grown-up children. Loree spends her time coaching, writing, learning, developing new projects, staying healthy and fit, and just overall enjoying the fantastic adventure of life.

For more information about Loree's coaching services or to obtain forms or worksheets you can visit her website at www.loreebischoff.com.

Comments and inquiries can be mailed to:

Loree Bischoff
PO Box 1195
Cody, WY 82414

or emailed to: loree@loreebischoff.com

16953708R00062

Printed in Great Britain
by Amazon